THE PHOENIX
AT THE FOUNTAIN

Images of Woman and Eternity
in Lactantius's *Carmen de Ave Phoenice*
and the Old English *Phoenix*

Carol Falvo Heffernan

DELAWARE

NEWARK: University of Delaware Press
LONDON AND TORONTO: Associated University Presses

PR
1750
. H44
1987

Associated University Presses
440 Forsgate Drive
Cranbury, NJ 08512

Associated University Presses
25 Sicilian Avenue
London WC1A 2QH, England

Associated University Presses
2133 Royal Windsor Drive
Unit 1
Mississauga, Ontario
Canada L5J 1K5

The paper used in this publication meets the requirements
of the American National Standard for Permanence of Paper
for Printed Library Materials Z39.48-1984.

Library of Congress Cataloging-in-Publication Data

Heffernan, Carol Falvo.
  The phoenix at the fountain.

  Bibliography: p.
  Includes index.
  1. Phoenix (Anglo-Saxon poem)   2. Lactantius,
ca. 240-ca. 320.   De ave Phoenice.   3. Phoenix
(Mythical bird) in literature.   4. Fountains in
literature.   5. Women in literature.   6. Initiation
rites in literature.   7. Human reproduction in
literature.   8. Women—Rites and ceremonies.
9. Literature, Comparative—Anglo-Saxon and Latin.
10. Literature, Comparative—Latin and Anglo-Saxon.
I. Title.
PR1750.H44   1988   829'.1   86-40368
ISBN 0-87413-313-0 (alk. paper)

Printed in the United States of America

THE PHOENIX
AT THE FOUNTAIN

FOR TOM

CONTENTS

ILLUSTRATIONS

ACKNOWLEDGMENTS

Most of this study was written during a leave of absence under the auspices of the Rutgers University Faculty Academic Study Program. Some of the preliminary research, aided by a Rutgers Research Council Summer Fellowship, was conducted at the New York Academy of Medicine. I am also indebted to Rutgers University for providing a grant toward the expenses of obtaining photographs and preparing the manuscript.

The collections of various libraries have facilitated the research for this book. Apart from the New York Academy of Medicine, I am especially grateful to the New York Public Library and to the libraries of Columbia University and Cornell University. The last is to be thanked for having extended borrowing privileges to me during three successive summers when I vacationed in Aurora, New York. I am also pleased to express my gratitude for having had the rich resources of the Lecky and Berkeley libraries at my disposal while I was doing research at Trinity College, Dublin. Many librarians have assisted me in locating illustrations from manuscripts housed in the collections of their institutions. Acknowledgments to the institutions for permission to publish illustrations from their holdings appear in the illustrative matter, but I would here like to thank several librarians for their aid: Mrs. J. Crowfoot Payne of the Ashmolean Museum, Oxford; Dr. Klaus Helfrich of the Museum für Völkerkunde, Berlin; Mr. Pierre Janin of the Bibliothèque Nationale, Paris; and Mr. A. C. D. Robinson of the British Library, London. To the photographic skills of Mr. Peter Rogers I owe the plate of the font at St. Mary's Church (Stafford, England).

Several people have read all or parts of this manuscript at various stages of its preparation, and I have profited from their suggestions and advice. At a very early stage in the development of the study, Professor Charles Owen, perhaps unwittingly, encouraged me to keep at it by allowing that I "got a lot right." Dr. David Burnley provided more support than he realized by inviting me to try out what became chapter 5 at a meeting of the History of the English Language Society at the University of Sheffield in spring 1981. Professors Alan Gaylord, Norman Blake, Joseph Pheifer, Mary Carruthers, Richard Levin, and Alain Renoir all provided helpful suggestions for the improvement of my work. I owe a special debt of gratitude to two colleagues who gave generously of advice, encouragement, and friendship: Professors Ann C. Watts and Henry Christian. I feel especially grateful to Professor Chauncey Wood for his constant good sense and useful leads.

Much of chapter 5 originally appeared as an article, "The Old English *Phoenix:* A Reconsideration," *Neuphilologische Mitteilungen (NM),* 83 (1982): 239–54. Permission has been granted by *NM* to draw on that article. Thanks are also due to Boydell & Brewer Ltd. and to *Papers on Language & Literature (PLL)* for permission to reprint. Much of the Epilogue's discussion of *The Romance of the Rose* first appeared in *The Spirit of the Court,* edited by Glyn S. Burgess and Robert A. Taylor (Cambridge: D. S. Brewer, 1985), and the remarks on *The Parliament of Fowls,* also in the Epilogue, draw on part of "Wells and Streams in Three Chaucerian Gardens," *PLL* 15(1979): 339–56.

I am grateful to the Manchester University Press for permission to quote extensively from Norman Blake's edition of *The Phoenix* and to Oxford University Press for permission to use Charles W. Kennedy's translation of the poem, which appears in his *Early English Christian Poetry.*

My greatest debt is acknowledged in the dedication to this book.

PROLOGUE

The myth of the phoenix ranks among the most evocative inventions of the human imagination, reflecting humanity's immemorial desire to escape the limits of time, to win the second chance, to begin anew. Its story concerns the world of human values and especially the question of the meaning of our existence here on earth. "To rise like a phoenix from the ashes" is as common a metaphor for the idea of renewal as the Fountain of Youth, although the comparison is probably used as frequently by those who do not know the myth as by those who do.

Two high points in the West's literary treatment of the story of the phoenix are the late Latin *Carmen de Ave Phoenice* of Lactantius and the eighth-century Old English *Phoenix*. While the phoenix myth was known in the eastern Mediterranean and the Roman empire before Lactantius (A.D. 250–A.D. 325), Lactantius's poem, the Anglo-Saxon poem that adapts and expands it, and subsequent derivative writings have constituted the main conduits through which the symbol has come down to us. The two poems, therefore, may be thought of as *the* central statement of the phoenix myth and they unquestionably represent the most detailed poetic treatment of the myth that we have received.

As these two poems are the focus of the book that follows, the reader may wish to be reminded of the broad outlines of both. Lactantius's *Carmen de Ave Phoenice* begins with a description of the phoenix's grove on a high plateau in the East. Remote from man and blessed with temperate weather, the grove has at its center a fountain that overflows twelve months of the year. Here the phoenix follows a daily ritual of immersing itself in the fountain at dawn, flying up to a perch on a tall tree, and singing as the sun rises. This pattern of life continues for a thousand years until the old phoenix needs to renew itself. Then the phoenix takes flight to Syria where it seeks out a palm tree in which to die and recreate itself. After the old phoenix dies in flames ignited by the sun, the young phoenix evolves from the amassed ashes of its predecessor. When it becomes an adult, it shapes whatever remains of the dead phoenix into a ball and takes it to an altar in Heliopolis. A joyous host of birds gather around the fabulous bird and sculpt it in marble amidst singing and gift-giving. In general, the same order of events is followed by the first 380 lines of the Old English *Phoenix* whose source the *Carmen* is. It is not to my purpose, at this early stage, to compare the details of the first part of the Old English poem to the Latin, but suffice it to say that most of the changes serve to Christianize the poem or to lead the way to the allegorical interpretation offered by the second half of *The Phoenix.* Herein the major symbols of the preceding 380 lines are interpreted Christologically: i.e., the tree in which the phoenix builds its nest is likened to Christ; the phoenix is said to be a sign of Christ as well as of the resurrection of the body on the day of doom.

My fortuitous point of entry into the study of the two poems was an interest in medieval literary fountains.[1] In puzzling over the detail that marks the phoenix fountains off from the many *fons vitae* images I had studied—the monthly overflow—I found it reasonable to think of the image not merely as scriptural but as natural, especially since Lactantius may well have written the *Carmen* before his conversion to Christianity and since the suggestion of the physiological was very compelling. The problem set by the mysterious duodecimal overflow, one of Lactantius's innovations within the myth, led to the exploration of the possible menstrual connections of the phoenix fountains. This, in turn, led to the discovery that the fountains appear to be a part of an interconnected pattern of imagery that, for want of a better term, I call "gynecological imagery," a term to be understood in an extended sense to include images pertaining to female physiology as well as to rituals associated with puberty and birth. So fundamental is this perception of the imagery that it leads one to suspect that the phoenix's secular associations with restoration and renewal come from the gynecological suggestions. As for the religious allegory, even that seems to have a rich female dimension, for the Old English poem, as I hope to demonstrate in chapter 5, may be viewed as including a Marian range of meaning.

What I would propose about these two poems is that their most potent imagery draws on female initiation rites and early scientific theories connected with menstruation, conception, and birth. Although this proposal may be daring, it seems less so in the light of the theme of creation concentrated in the background of the phoenix myth (a subject explored in the first chapter). Thus far the anthropological and scientific dimensions of the poems have escaped the notice of scholars, both those who have enlarged our appreciation of the literary qualities of the Latin and Old English poems and those who have advanced our understanding of the phoenix myth. By exploring the neglected anthropological and scientific background of the poems' images, I hope to demonstrate that early views about female physiology and the scenario of female initiation rites constitute such pervasive forces in the poetry that we need to reevaluate our interpretation of the poems. Nonetheless, the subject of this book is not so much the text of the phoenix poems as it is a compartment of the human imagination from which issue now literary expressions, now behavioral expressions. This study is not literary criticism that draws support from another discipline on the order of psychological criticism and historical criticism; it is *not* anthropological criticism of the phoenix poems. It is, rather, a study that is cross-disciplinary to the extent that readers may as easily, depending on their bias, find it a novelty to see so much literature entering an anthropological discussion as they may to see so much anthropology entering a literary discussion. The reader used to conventional literary scholarship may be put off to find that the poems do not always come first. There is a reason. In this case the poems come *with*, not before.

This approach answers the question of why the phoenix fountains overflow twelve times yearly and deepens our understanding of the relationship of the feminine to other medieval fountains: those, for example, that appear in Chrétien de Troyes's *Yvain*, in several narratives by Geoffrey Chaucer, and in Guillaume de Lorris and Jean de Meun's *Romance of the Rose*. Other details of the phoenix's behavior that have been approached, heretofore, from the exclusively literary point of view of religious allegory may also still be viewed as somewhat mysterious. In uncovering the anthropological and scientific levels of the poems, this examination enables the reader to view not only the fountain but the phoenix's seclusion, its ritual bath and drinking at the fountain, the escort that accompanies it, and the bird's second cycle of life in the Anglo-Saxon poem, as well as other similarly distinctive actions, in a new light. Moreover, the study may serve as a provocation to new research that will help us understand more fully the universal appeal of fountains in garden settings and that may further illustrate why images with an obviously pagan foundation could so easily be transformed for the use of Christian allegory. It is also to be hoped that the work will give impetus to more cross-disciplinary research in medieval studies. The whole "gynecological" reading of the poems is the fruit of analysis and comparison; whether or not that motif makes them more interesting to feminists, the reading is necessitated by found evidence and did not grow out of any a priori thesis.

The book's methodology came about through a recognition in the phoenix poems of female physiological elements that naturally suggested certain discoveries anthropologists had made about female initiation rites as well as classical and medieval notions of conception and embryology. Following these clues has been like prying open the door of the pyramid: the extent of the supporting evidence was overwhelming. The novelty of the discovery has necessarily entailed a certain novelty of approach, for the study rests mainly on three bases: literature; myth and theology; and anthropology and early science. The study could not be a purely literary one, for the two poems are being viewed as having been generated by a process that is more than literary.

In the following chapters I propose to examine the pertinent elements of the Latin and Old English poems more or less in the order in which they present themselves and to observe that there are easily distinguishable Menstrual, Conception, and Birth Sequences of imagery in both poems. I will also suggest that this radically new approach to the poems affects traditional allegorical interpretation and illuminates the meaning of other medieval literary fountains.

But before I begin, let me anticipate a few questions the reader may already have. First, could Lactantius, a third-century church father, teacher of rhetoric in the reign of Diocletian, have any knowledge of the initiation rituals I am about to discuss?[2] I think so, particularly since he began life as a native of Africa and a pagan. Although as a Roman African he was probably born somewhere in North Africa, he was not necessarily cut off from the practices of the "traditional religions" of peoples to the south, east, and west. And by "traditional religions" I mean to refer, as do T. O. Ranger and I. N. Kimambo, to those ceremonies that seem to be part of a "timeless ethnographic present," unlike the "historic" religions of Islam and Christianity.[3] As early as the time of the pharaohs, there is evidence of movement from the north toward the interior of Africa. J. H. Breasted, in his *Ancient Records of Egypt*, records four early accounts of journeys to the south made by a nobleman of Aswan in the sixth dynasty (about 2340 B.C.); in one of these, it is clear that a native has been brought back to Egypt: "a dancing dwarf of the god from the land of the spirits."[4] It is known, moreover, that before the middle of the first millenium, trans-African trails crossed between the Middle Nile and the region of Lake Chad.[5] It was probably along such a trail that the technique of smelting iron traveled from the north to west-central Africa.[6] An example of travel southward from North Africa in Christian times (A.D. 60) is offered by the mariner's handbook, *The Periplus of the Erythraean Sea*, written by an Egyptian seafarer. He writes of the advantages there are to be had in traveling south of the Nile in an area believed to be modern Tanzania. In his account, he says of it that, despite hazards, "there is ivory in great quantity, and tortoise shell."[7] Apart from the lure of ivory, voyages were made down the East African coast to acquire aromatic gums from the region of Cape Guardafui.[8] There has been a notable reported find of Ptolemaic and Roman coins in the southern part of the Somali coast that has been put forth as evidence of the kind of trade of which the *Periplus* informs us.[9] This find is believed to be in the area of the early settlement of the northeastern Bantu who later spread south and west.[10]

Even if we grant that there is extant evidence of movement among the different regions of Africa in early times that would have made it possible for accounts of native practices and, indeed, even for their practitioners to be carried northwards to higher civilizations, what bearing would descriptions of rites observed in the nineteenth and twentieth centuries have on the early ones? The notion that modern phenomena can teach us about the past is nothing new. In 1871 E. B. Taylor wrote, "If we choose out . . . things which have altered little in a long course of centuries, we may draw a picture where there shall be scarce a hand's breadth difference between an English ploughman and a negro of central Africa."[11] Along these lines recent field work by Jeff Opland among the Xhosa- and Zulu-speaking peoples of South Africa has uncovered a significant analogue for Old English oral poetry. Pointing out that many of the extant Anglo-Saxon manuscripts contain eulogistic poetry, the kind that is at the heart of southeastern Bantu poetic tradition, Opland's examination of the African poetry demonstrates that the "study of living poetic traditions can teach us much about how oral poetry lived and operated in societies remote in time."[12] Initiation rites have never been studied historically, although they are the subject of lively anthropological examination that, unfortunately for this question, treats them as part of a continuous ethnographic present. This stance, however, may not be far from the mark, as it is generally believed that "ceremonies of initiation were of all aspects of society the least susceptible to change."[13] So reflective are they of the timeless concerns and shared beliefs of agricultural settlements that rituals of initiation in countries geographically far removed from one another contain striking resemblances. What Cleanth Brooks once said of poetry applies equally well to ritual: "It is a matter of fact that modern readers can appreciate *Antigone* as a piece of literature and can make meaningful comparisons between it as a drama and the dramas of William Shakespeare or Thomas Otway or Tennessee Williams."[14] This is because of the essential unifying humanity that transcends the differences that separate individuals of various cultures. Viewed as inductive evidence, the extent of the parallels between the symbols of Lactantius's *Carmen* (and the first half of the Old English poem that draws directly on it) and the rites described by anthropologists may be taken as an indication not only that the late Latin poem reflects aspects of puberty and birth rituals but that indeed, early ceremonies must have been similar to their more modern counterparts.

And lastly, the reader might wonder if Lactantius had these rites in mind as he composed or if he merely inherited a myth that, in its received state, reflected female initiation rites. Given the fact that no version of the myth is so full and so elaborately detailed as Lactantius's account and that he introduces, from the point of view of my thesis, crucial elements that appear in the story for the first time, it is hard to imagine that chance and not conscious intention accounts for the parallels that I am about to discuss. The problem of intentionality is greater in the case of the Old English poem, but there is reason to believe, as chapter 5 demonstrates, that the anonymous poet was cognizant of the feminine dimension of his poem even though he is silent about it—perhaps even suppresses it—in the explicit second half of the poem.

THE PHOENIX
AT THE FOUNTAIN

1
INTRODUCTION

AT the start I would present, as if putting a legend in the corner of a map, a few details concerning an analogue to the phoenix, the Egyptian *benu* bird. The *benu*, mentioned in the Egyptian *Book of the Dead* and other sources, is a mythical heron-like bird associated with the sun, sun worship, and the Egyptian city of the sun, Heliopolis; most important, the *benu* has the power to regenerate itself. The two main versions of the phoenix myth in classical and early Christian literature, both of which have as their themes restored existence and restored vitality, look like natural outgrowths of *benu* mythology.

According to one tradition the new phoenix is generated from the decaying remains of the phoenix that has died in a nest of aromatic herbs.[1] The young bird then carries his predecessor to the altar of the Sun-god in Heliopolis. The link between the phoenix and Egyptian myth often occurs in the second, more widespread, tradition, according to which the phoenix dies after its term of life by attracting the heat of the sun's rays to its nest of aromatics and then burning in the flames.[2] The new phoenix first appears as a worm that creeps out of the ashes, grows in due course to a bird, and flies away. Many authors writing in this tradition locate the actual burning of the phoenix at the altar in Heliopolis, the site of the *benu*'s conflagration.

The associations with Heliopolis and the Temple of the Sun draw attention to the relationship between the phoenix and the sun implicit in both principal versions of the myth. It is reasonable to connect the phoenix's periodic rebirth with the daily course of rising and setting of the sun, the maker of time. The fact that Heliopolis appears in both European versions of the myth suggests that the story has an Egyptian origin.

But it is not necessary to determine definitively the bird's Egyptian origins to see that there are several elements in the symbolism of the *benu* that harmonize with the central theme of the phoenix myth, rebirth. The *benu* had played a role in ancient Egyptian thinking about the primeval act of creation. In the beginning, when Atum created the world and the primeval hill was the first thing to rise out of the waters of chaos, the *benu* perched on the hill, and its first flight across the sky marked the beginning of time.³ Because of its role in this creation myth, the *benu*, signifying the return to a new beginning, the start of a New Era, was a natural symbol for the Sothic period. Robert Graves explains the meaning of the Sothic year this way:

> The Egyptians had no leap year: every year the fragment of a day which was left over at New Year was saved up, until finally after 1460 years, called a Sothic Year, the fragments amounted to a whole year; the fixed festivals which had become more and more displaced as the centuries went by . . . fetched up again where they had originally stood; and a whole year could be intercalated in the annals.⁴

The *benu's* association with the Sothic year both links it with the regulation of time, making it, as Graves says, "a calendar beast," and shows it to be a sign of the renewal of all things.

Another revealing connection between the *benu* and the theme of rebirth is its relationship to a dead person's quest for immortality. The eighty-third chapter of the *Book of the Dead* contains a spell for transforming a dead person into a *benu*, enabling him or her to fly to the eternal land beyond.⁵ The magical formula begins, "I fly up as one in the beginning *(paw.ty)* and become *Khepri.*"⁶ *Khepri*, the dung-beetle, is, like the *benu*, a form of the sun god who was born spontaneously at the creation. The incantation is clearly based on the metaphor of the primeval flight of the *benu* bird and is intended to raise the dead from their tombs and convey them across the sky beyond the world of time. It is natural that in Egypt, where the *benu* was intimately involved in the myth of creation, the bird should become a vehicle for the desire of the dead to transcend time. Death and resurrection are at the core of the two principal versions of the phoenix myth; although it cannot be established conclusively that the European phoenix myth developed from the Egyptian *benu* myth, the connection seems sound.

We may infer that the *benu* and phoenix myths are at the least analogous. But, in the light of all the evidence that anthropology and the history of physiology have to shed on the meaning of the phoenix, this inference is just a first step along the road. The phoenix itself has, as we shall see in chapter 2, traits of another mythical bird, this time a bird whose function it is to attend the beginnings of menstruation. The conclusion that the phoenix is a literary relative of this bird is supported by the ease with which the phoenix poems' subordinate images and narrative elements identify with primitive rites and early theories related to menarche, conception, and birth. Hence the proposal I outlined above to distinguish in the two phoenix poems the material composing what I call the Menstrual, Conception, and Birth Sequences. As the poems advance, these elements may be seen to do their work sometimes allusively and sometimes systematically and logically. The elements are: first, the bird itself, its bathing (fountain, water), its seclusion, and its life among trees, all of which relate to menstrual ritual; second, the sun and song, which constitute the two main elements of the Conception Sequence; and third, the sun (heat, fire), the fumigation, the ball of ashes, the apple and worm, the seed, the escort and ring, and the manifestation, all of which relate to theories and rites connected with birth. At a few points in the poem symbols from one sequence appear also in another. The image of the sun, for example, is an element of both the Conception and Birth Sequences.

Since the heart of the discussion that follows concerns these three sequences, Menarche, Conception, and Birth, a few words about each may serve to introduce the examinations of them in chapters 2, 3, and 4.

Menarche

For reasons which become clearer as we talk about the bird in the light of primitive beliefs and customs surrounding menarche, considering the bird image will mean considering as well the crocodile symbolism of primitive rites and the blood references of the Old English poem. Early in the poems we are shown a fountain in the garden where the phoenix dwells that has the suggestive property of overflowing twelve times annually. Since the well or spring is an archetypal symbol of the womb—an idea underscored by the fact that the Egyptian hieroglyph for "well full of water" also means "vulva"[7]—it is reasonable to associate the imaginary fountain in the poems with those fountains that do, in fact, overflow twelve times a year. What makes this identification especially significant is the behavior of the phoenix at the fountain. The bird's ritual immersion in what has the cyclical quality of menstrual blood completes a picture that has been presented in myths of primitive peoples who even today, in effect, live at the Paleolithic stage of human history. The phenomenon of the blood that flows from the female genitals at regular intervals is explained in several such societies as a wound resulting from the attack of a bird or, sometimes, a crocodile. A series of carved wooden figures in the Berlin Ethnographical Museum offers fantastic graphic illustration of the supposed genesis of the menstrual flow. Unfortunately the two carvings that most pointedly represent this phenomenon were lost during World War II.[8] My photographs of them come not from originals but from reproductions by the ethnographers, Max Bartels and Hermann Ploss. A wood carving ascribed by them to New Britain,[9] but which Dr. Klaus Helfrich attributes to New Ireland, shows a bird with a large curved beak drawing a red object from the figure's exposed vulva. In *Woman's Mysteries*, Esther Harding points out that ancient representa-

Carved wooden female figure from New Ireland showing a bird drawing
something out of the genitals. Berlin, Museum für Völkerkunde (carving lost
during World War II). *(From Hermann H. Ploss and Max Bartels,* Woman: An
Historical, Gynaecological and Anthropological Compendium, *ed. Eric Dingwall (London: William Heinemann, 1935), 1: fig. 466.)*

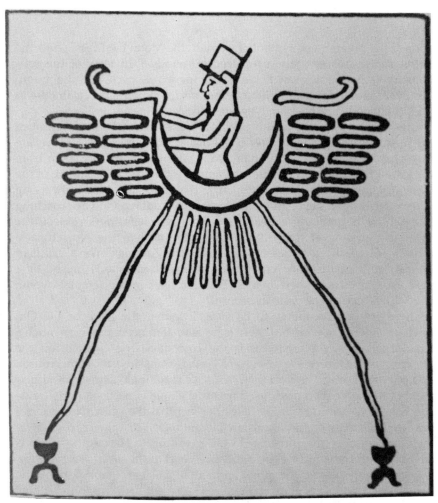

Assyrian Winged Moon from an Assyrian cylinder, probably eighteenth dynasty. From a drawing by Esther Harding, *Woman's Mysteries* (New York: Harper & Row, 1971), Fig. 16. *(By permission of C. G. Jung Foundation. Photo courtesy of General Research and Humanities Division, The New York Public Library, Astor, Lenox, and Tilden Foundations.)*

tions of the preeminent symbol of woman, the Moon Goddess, show the horns of the crescent moon replaced by wings.[10] In view of the relationship early peoples saw between the menstrual cycle and the moon, this avian moon appears to tie together bird, woman, and catamenia as does the wood carving from New Ireland.[11]

Other carvings in the Ethnographical Museum also bear on primitive myth surrounding the mysterious flow of the catamenia. There are carvings, for example, from Suam, New Guinea, on planks taken from huts used to sequester girls menstruating for the first time. In one of the most striking, a female figure similar to that in the New Ireland carving is depicted under siege, this time by two crocodiles. One approaching from above is grabbing a headdress from which feathers project; the other is thrusting at the vulva as does the bird in the New Ireland carving. Similarly, a belief of the Luvale of Zambia links a reptilian creature to menstruation. The Luvale believe menarche is caused by a snakelike creature known as a *chisumi* that lives in the female's womb and with which every woman is born.[12]

There are no crocodiles, to be sure, in either the Latin or the Old English phoenix poems, but there is no animal in myth that is as much a counterpart of the phoenix as is the crocodile. In a passage on the phoenix in the Greek *Physiologus of Vienna*, translated by Jean Hubaux and Maxime Leroy, we read that: "C'est sa mandibule supérieure qui se meut et non celle d'en dessous: il ne soulève que la partie supérieure de son bec."[13] R. Van den Broek takes the fact that the phoenix can move only its upper jaw as "an unmistakable indication that the crocodile was the companion of the phoenix,"[14] for according to Herodotus—who is credited with transmitting the phoenix legend to the west—and Aristotle—who propounded the most influential ancient theory about the generative function of the catamenia—the crocodile is the only animal unable to move its lower jaw.

Another recognized feature that the crocodile has in common with the phoenix is that in Egypt both are sun animals. Clement of Alexandria notes that some Egyptian symbols "show the sun on a ship, others on a crocodile."[15] Plate XI (nos. 4 and 5) of Van den Broek's study of the myth depicts the *benu* bird standing on what appears to be a crocodile; evidently the *benu* is here a representation of the sun god, Ra. The importance of the sun in theories of generation, which will be discussed later in the present study, heightens the significance of its being symbolically common to crocodile and phoenix.

Crocodile and bird are central symbols of female puberty rituals in many primitive societies. Here it is particularly appropriate to consider African rituals since the weighty scholarship linking the origins of the phoenix legend to Egypt points the way to Africa and since the author of

Wood carving from a menstrual hut in Suam, New Guinea, showing a female
under siege by two crocodiles. Berlin, Museum für Völkerkunde (like Plate 1,
lost). *(From Ploss and Bartels, 1: fig. 467.)*

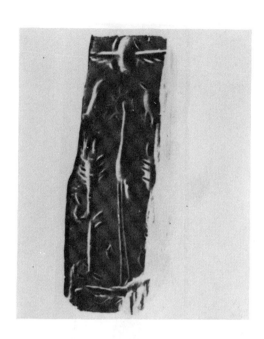

Egyptian amulets with the *benu*-bird standing on the back of a crocodile. *From Collection Seyrig, by permission of the Kelsey Museum of Ancient and Medieval Archaeology, Ann Arbor, Michigan, and Cabinet des medailles et antiquités [Fr. 2884], by permission of the Bibliothèque Nationale.)*

the earlier of the two phoenix poems, Lactantius, was born of heathen parents in Africa. In the next chapter we will examine these rituals to see what, besides crocodile and bird, they contain in common from one society to another and in common with the imagery of the two poems.

I shall argue, then, that the phoenix of the two poems, bathing in the fountain of the duodecimal flow, may be a relative of the mythic menstrual bird believed to have brought about the beginning of menstruation in woman. We may add to this possible connection between phoenix and woman the additional, more general identification made in ancient times between birds and the feminine principle. This identification will allow us to view the phoenix of the poems as not merely in touch with an intimate aspect of woman, by virtue of its position in the womb of Mother Earth, but as actually partaking of the feminine nature and thus able to give birth, the most female of functions.

Conception and Birth

In a recent study of the representations of gods and goddesses in ancient art, Marija Gimbutas discusses a large group of Neolithic figurines sculpted to represent the concept of the Bird Goddess.[16] For a long time archaeologists erroneously adopted the term *steatopygous* for the standing and stooping figurines because the enlarged, egg-shaped buttocks suggested the abnormal condition that is occasionally found in women. The objects are now recognized as anthropomorphized birds that contain the cosmic egg from which gods were supposed to arise according to ancient Egyptian, Babylonian, Hindu, and Greek creation myths. Besides the story of Creation in which the *benu* plays a part, there was an earlier ancient Egyptian myth of the Nile goose, called "the Chatterer," creator of the universe, that laid the cosmic egg.[17] Since it may be disconcerting to find more than one species of bird playing a part in Egyptian creation myths, it is important to note a point made by R. T. Rundle-Clark in his study of the phoenix as an Egyptian religious symbol:

> Most of the great culture areas possess one or more of these magic creatures . . . it is almost immaterial whether the bird is natural or mythical or to what species it belongs. In Egyptian religion the same thing is true, the bird role is quite typical although the kind of bird changes from text to text.[18]

It should also be borne in mind, when we come later to consider the question of the indeterminate gender of the phoenix, that the Neolithic sculptural realizations of the Bird Goddesses have both female egg-shaped buttocks and long phallic necks, suggesting a fusion of the

Marble sculpture of Bird Goddess with long phallic neck and pronounced buttocks. Slightly stooping position reminiscent of a bird. Attica, Greece. *(By permission of the Museum of Eleusis.)*

Different views of a Bird Goddess from Macedonia, c. 5800 B.C. From Marija Gimbutas, *The Gods and Goddesses of Old Europe* (Berkeley: University of California Press, 1974), Figs. 113–15, from her 1969 excavation. *(By permission of the University of California Press and Marija Gimbutas. Photo courtesy of Caroline Minionis.)*

Bird Goddess from Achilleion, Thessaly, Greece, c. 6000 B.C. Parting of human hairdo combined with birdlike beak visible in leftmost view. Gimbutas, Fig. 1. (excavated in 1973 by M. Gimbutas). *(By permission of University of California Press and Marija Gimbutas. Photo courtesy of Caroline Minionis.)*

sexes.[19] We are reminded by Mircea Eliade that "life springs from an over-fullness, from a wholeness. . . . So, if we say that the Supreme Beings of the primitives are—or were—androgyne, this in no way excludes their 'masculinity' or their 'femininity.' "[20] Despite the suggestion of androgyny in the Bird Goddess, there is no doubt that she primarily represents the feminine principle, as is demonstrated, for example, by Gimbutas, who discusses types of the anthropomorphic bird found in many regions depicted as a nurse or mother holding a baby.[21] The avian nature of the Bird Goddess figurines Gimbutas describes is represented in the characteristic forward-leaning, stooping posture. According to Gimbutas, features of the Bird Goddess may be discerned in Greek terra-cottas of Aphrodite, Goddess of Love, dating from the sixth and fifth centuries B.C. The sculptures depict her as "flying through the air, standing or sitting on a goose or being accompanied by three geese."[22] In a discussion of early representations of the Moon Goddess, Harding also speaks of the relationship between birds and several of the goddesses of the Greek pantheon. She observes that doves and pigeons usually appear in the temples of Aphrodite and that, on a box of Cypselus, Diana is portrayed as winged—also characteristic of Artemis, who frequently appears with curved wings.[23] Although, we tend to associate Diana and Artemis with chastity, they were in early days thought of as goddesses of fecundity and childbearing.[24] Diana watched over childbirth and was called "Opener of the Womb," and, according to Euripides, Artemis never spoke to childless women.[25] These comparatively late representations indicate that the conception of the Neolithic Bird Goddesses either was not lost ánd stayed on to enrich the art of ancient Europe or was from the start a reflection of an archetype of the human psyche. In this light the feminine dimension of the phoenix poems about to be explored may be viewed as evidence that the influence of the Bird Goddess is felt in early poetry as well as in the plastic arts.[26]

The phoenix of the Latin and Old English poems is a creator: out of the ashes of its dead self it makes another self. As is most clearly seen in the allegorical second half of the Old English poem, Christian thinkers interpreted this reborn bird as the symbol of the resurrection of the flesh and the beginning of a new life in eternity. The attainment of another mode of being was viewed naturally by the Christian as equivalent to being born a second time. Primitive peoples take precisely the same view of the girl who has undergone the process of female initiation: she has been reborn into fecundity and adult personality—"reborn," because to attain this level the girl has died to the state of childhood. Eliade clarifies the meaning of the process of female puberty rituals:

> Initiation is equivalent to a change of level, to the passing out of one mode of being into another; the young girl is brutally separated from the profane world; she undergoes a transformation of a spiritual character which, like all transformations, implies an experience of death. . . . But what is in question is always *a death to something which has to be surpassed.* . . . One dies to be transformed and attain to a higher level of existence. In the case of the girls, this is death to the indistinct and amorphous state of childhood.[27]

It was easier to determine for girls than for boys when the process of initiation should begin, for primitive peoples, like their modern counterparts, knew that the occurrence of menarche meant a girl had become fecund and was ready to learn about her creative role. For primitive peoples the birth process was sacred because it had a cosmogonic valency;[28] it was a microcosmic version of the primeval act of creation by which the world began: "In the end, all kinds of making are homologized by being identified with the supreme example of the 'made,' the cosmogony."[29] When we view it from this perspective, we can see that what happens to the woman in parturition may have, in the case of the Egyptian creation myth, a parallel in the *benu* that alights on the primeval mound at the beginning of time. Correspondingly in art, we may see a parallel in the terra-cotta figurines of the Bird Goddess and, most important for the purpose of this study, a parallel in certain elements of the narrative structure and individual images of Lactantius's *Carmen de Ave Phoenice* and the Old English *Phoenix*. These elements and images, as the following chapters will demonstrate, borrow not only from the early history of embryology but from the imagery and initiatory themes of female puberty ritual. As we see most clearly in the Old English poem, which, there can be no doubt, was written by a Christian poet, initiatory patterns having once lost their (pagan) religious reality, can become revalorized as literary motifs in a Christian context. What Eliade observes about the use of initiation themes in Arthurian romance literature applies, even though the scenarios are not puberal, to the initiation patterns in the poems we will consider: "They . . .deliver their spiritual message on a different plane of human experience, by addressing themselves directly to the imagination."[30]

It cannot be said, as C. S. Lewis says of R. S. Loomis's derivation of the Grail from the Celtic cornucopia, that there is an "abyss" between the phoenix poems and the features of female initiation ritual (or, for that matter, early generative theory) and that their "inward" sides differ.[31] The anthropological and scientific materials drawn out of the poems in the following chapters reinforce a primary imaginative theme, that of transcendence. Female initiation ritual moves the child out of herself to achieve a new level of being. The phoenix of the poems transcends the limitations of time in this world by being reborn and entering another one. Even the early history of embryology, as it sheds light on 'specific images in the poems, demonstrates ultimately how ancient and medieval scientists evolved theories to explain how human beings transcend themselves by giving birth to a new generation. As I shall show in detail in subsequent chapters, the Latin and Anglo-Saxon poets have imaginatively combined ritual and science to realize a more powerful aesthetic effect. Although these materials drawn from female initiation ceremonies and theories of generation may seem far removed, at first glance, from a poetic rendering of the myth of the phoenix's rebirth, the process of transcendence is at the core of all of them. These anthropological and scientific materials are far less at odds with their ostensible subject than the diverse materials out of which John Donne, for example, shaped his poetry.

From the point of view of my thesis, which draws attention to the phoenix's role as a creator, there are several findings of modern scholars of the myth, apart from those discussed earlier in this chapter, that harmonize with my own. Besides the possible descent of the phoenix from the Egyptian *benu*, associated with creation myths and renewal of all things at the Sothic Year, there are several associations that seem to point to the theme of generation: namely, ties between the phoenix and Venus (paralleled by links between the *benu* and Sothis-Isis) as well as between the phoenix and the Virgin Mary.

In a fragment of a poem preserved by Flavius Sosipater Charisius,[32] the phoenix speaks of itself as a follower of Venus, here simultaneously the Goddess of Love and the morning star that appears at dawn before the sun. The poem is *Pterygion Phoenicis* by Laevius, a poet living about 100 B.C. It is an emblematic poem, the different line lengths of which are believed to represent the object described—the wings of the phoenix:

> Venus ⟨o⟩ amoris altrix,
> genetrix cupiditatis,
> mihi quae diem serenum
> hilarula praepandere cresti,
> opesculae tuae ac ministrae.[33]

> [O Venus, who keeps love alive,
> mother of longing and desire,
> it is you who favors me,
> your little maid servant,
> and spreads out a calm day
> in front of me.]

The wings of the phoenix were a mysterious subject for description because, according to the *Greek Apocalypse of Pseudo-Baruch*, they were inscribed with words explaining the bird's origin.[34] H. de la Ville de Mirmont concludes that the phoenix itself speaks the words,[35] and it is notable that the phoenix employs the feminine gender; this indicates that Laevius regarded the bird as female, an idea that makes it all the easier to infer from the fragmentary verses that the phoenix is consecrated to Venus (as well as to the sun).[36] Hubaux and Leroy make this inference,[37] and point for parallel evidence to lines 17–20 of Claudian's *Phenix*, wherein the phoenix appears to carry the morning star on its head:

> Arcanum radiant oculi iubar; igneus ora
> Cingit honos. Rutilo cognatum vertice sidus
> Attollit cristatus apex tenebrasque serena
> Luce secat.[38]

> [The eyes radiate a hidden brightness.
> The fiery glory surrounds its face.
> Its tufted crest lifts the kindred heavens
> on its red summit and cuts the
> shadows with serene light.]

To reinforce the Venus-phoenix link one might point to lines from the poem, *Romulea*, by the African poet Dracontius that bring together not dawn-phoenix-Venus but dawn-phoenix-Cupid (the son of Venus and God of Love). The context is that Venus has sent Hymen to find Cupid who, she says, cannot be far since the waves are billowing as if the sun were about to rise over the ocean. And, indeed, just then the God of Love appears:

> . . . per cuncta videres
> scintillare diem, volitant super aequora flammae.
> sic, ubi puniceos rutilans Aurora capillos
> Phoenix, sola genus, senio lassata vetusto,
> cinnama cui folium nardum tus balsama amomum
> informant post saecla pyram reditura, sepulchrum
> conscendit factura rogos et verberat alas
> ut flammas adsciscat avis (sic nascitur ignis
> ante alitem ambrosios iam consumpturus odores):
> sic puer Idalius spargebat plausibus ignes:[39]

(100–109)

> [Everywhere the day is seen to sparkle;
> Flames fly over the wavetops
> As when Aurora turns her hair deep red.
> The phoenix, alone of its kind and tired
>   from its great old age
> Takes cinnamon, nard leaves, incense and
>   balsam

To build the pyre to which it returns
          after centuries.
It ascends to make its tomb and fans the
          flame with its wings.
As the bird takes the flames unto himself
(So the flame is born before the bird, all
          the more ambrosial for the scents it will consume),
Thus the Idalian boy scatters with wingbeats
          the flames.]

Thus Dracontius, like Laevius and Claudian, by uniting the phoenix with dawn and a God of Love, makes of the phoenix a bird of beginnings.

In Egypt, it was not Venus, the morning star, with which the *benu* was associated but the dog star, Sothis. Tacitus stated that the phoenix *(-benu)* appeared in Egypt at intervals of 1,461 years,[40] the Sothic Period, whose symbol the *benu* was.[41] It was distinguished by the fact that the first day of the standard 365-day Egyptian year coincided with the solar year of 365¼ days. The period is named for the star Sothis because the star rose on New Year's Day, at the first flooding of the Nile, for the first four years of the cycle.[42] During the ordinary calendar year of the ancient Egyptians the date of the heliacal rising of Sothis coincided fairly closely with the start of the rising of the Nile and regularly marked the beginning of the year.[43] Thus, linked with the flooding of the Nile and the renewal of vegetation, Sothis was held in particular esteem. As Hubaux and Leroy put the matter, "Les Égyptiens établissaient donc une relation de cause à effet, non pas directement entre l'inondation et le moment où le soleil atteint son maximum chaleur, mais bien entre le débordement du Nil et le lever de Sothis."[44]

The star Sothis was consecrated[45] to the Egyptian goddess Isis, not infrequently called Isis-Sothis. I am not aware of any direct relationship between the *benu* and the goddess beyond their mutual symbolic links to the star Sothis, but representations of birds did appear in temples dedicated to Isis. These, however, are generally said to represent the ibis, a symbol of morning,[46] the best known example of which is probably that recovered from the Temple of Isis destroyed in the eruption of Vesuvius in 79 A.D. Isis, like Venus, is a Goddess of Love. Plutarch says of her: "For Isis is the feminine [principle] of nature and that which is capable of receiving the whole of genesis; in virtue of which she has been called 'Nurse' and 'all Receiving' by Plato."[47] Sir Wallis Budge is said to have interpreted the symbol of Isis as "a womb with its dependent ovaries, meaning that the very nature of Isis is expressed in her generative power."[48] In public rituals celebrating Isis, she was represented by a vase of water,[49] and the typical statue of the goddess generally depicts her as a mother holding a child.[50] Indeed, many such ancient statues have been taken over by Christian communities who regard them as representations of the Virgin Mary holding Jesus—an interesting fact in light of my concluding linkage: that between the appearance of the phoenix and the virgin birth.

A fragment of a fifth-century Coptic sermon on the Virgin Mary and the death of Christ, dealing almost entirely with the phoenix, is preserved in the University of Utrecht and provides the newest information uncovered about the phoenix. After a long discussion of the phoenix, there is a clear indication that the sermon was part of a celebration of the *Commemoration of Mary*:

> Let us return to our subject and glorify the holy Virgin Mary, for we are gathered together in her sacred place because it is the day of her Commemoration, on which we celebrate a feast for her![51]

The most significant event celebrated in this Marian feast was the event that distinguished the life of Mary: the virgin birth of Christ. According to the Coptic text, the last known appearance of the phoenix marked the birth of Jesus in Bethlehem:

> in this year now the Son of God was born in Bethlehem. And on the day that the priest Zechariah was killed, they installed the priest Simeon in his place. The phoenix burned itself on the pinnacle of the temple in Jerusalem. On the eighth day after the holy Virgin had brought forth our Saviour, she took him with Joseph to the temple in order to make a sacrifice for him as the firstborn, [and] he was named Jesus. From that moment now no one has ever seen that bird to this day.[52]

The appearance of the phoenix must certainly signal that with the birth of Christ a New Era begins; but that the bird appears at the moment of a birth—a virgin one like its own—seems to me significant in itself. Indeed, it seems that in this Coptic sermon read at the Commemoration of Mary there is as much emphasis on her and an amazing birth as on Christ, the fruit of that birth. Likewise, the famous phoenix mosaic in the triumphal arch in the Church of St. Maria in Trastevere, Rome, celebrates Mary rather than Christ. Whereas the phoenix is often said to represent the Resurrection of Christ, this phoenix mosaic is usually interpreted as a symbolic representation of the Virgin Mary.[53] The use of the phoenix, however, as a symbol for Mary is fairly common in the later Middle Ages and Renaissance. But the Coptic sermon and the specific reading my findings will imply for the Old English *Phoenix* suggest both an earlier manifestation of the phoenix's assocation with Mary and a larger role for maternal and feminine principles than was previously

Emblem of Isis. From Harding, Fig. 4 (her drawing). *(By permission of C. G. Jung Foundation. Photo courtesy of General Research and Humanities Division, The New York Public Library, Astor, Lenox, and Tilden Foundations.)*

thought to exist in early medieval Christian thought. In chapter 5, we will return to the possible Marian dimension of the phoenix symbol as it functions in the poem by the anonymous Anglo-Saxon poet. I hasten to stress, however, that my attention to this level of interpretation in the poem does not imply a rejection of the established Christological readings, some of them brilliant; my intent is merely to draw attention to a related parallel level in the poem.

The associations of the phoenix with Venus, Sothis-Isis, and the Virgin Mary seem to be at one with the context of past relationships of images that draw into the phoenix symbol. We will explore the generative content of this context in the following chapters.

2
THE MENSTRUAL SEQUENCE

IT has been argued that humanity's awe of the procreative power of women is the source of some of the most splendid inventions of the western imagination.[1] Not only are Lactantius's *Carmen de Ave Phoenice* and the Old English *Phoenix* embraced by this idea but the foundation on which I think their imagery rests indicates that preliterate peoples are not inferior to their civilized counterparts in their regard for the creative power of women.

Primitive peoples, like ancient and medieval scientific thinkers, thought of blood as a sign of that fecundity, for they were able to perceive that procreation could not take place before women began to menstruate. Thus the old African woman says to the young Chaga girls she will help initiate: "My children, the man of god has supplied a woman with the unction of fertility, the blood which comes once every month."[2] Because the appearance of menstrual bleeding is recognized as a sign of the girl's ability to bear children, the onset of menstruation is made the occasion of female initiation ceremonies.

We shall observe in this chapter that many of the symbols and actions of rituals celebrating menarche correspond to those I am calling the Menstrual Sequence in lines 1–43 of the *Carmen* and 1–119 of *The Phoenix*. The elements constituting the Menstrual Sequence that stand out for their relationship to female initiation rites are: the bird, bathing (fountain, water), seclusion, and trees. These parallel symbols and actions that I detect are archetypal, to be sure; nonetheless, it is possible that some of them may have been transmitted to Lactantius directly by life as it was lived in his day and as life patterns communicated themselves along such lines of diffusion as are discussed in the Prologue. Recall that his account introduces elements into the myth that appear for the first time. Moreover, no account of the story of the phoenix is as detailed as the version told by the African poet. And, perhaps more important than even the parallel elements, the occasion celebrated by the ritual and the story in the poems is the same: a transformation. Rites of transition mark a change of status, and the ritual-like actions of the bird conduct it to that fertile moment in which it renews itself. Old Bemba women who take charge of the initiation ceremony, called *chisungu*, in their tribe say the ritual is performed "to make the girl grow *(ukumukushaya)"*;[3] gradually in the course of the phoenix's bathing and sun-worship it comes of age, at which time the old bird dies and a new one is born. Death and birth are also brought together, in a sense, during the *chisungu*, as the sterile child dies and the fertile woman is born.

Bird

Before I discuss the bird symbol, an element both of female initiation rituals and of the Latin and Old English phoenix poems, more needs to be said about the bird's role—sometimes shared with a crocodile—in mythic explanations of the origin of menstruation and about the close relationship between the phoenix and the crocodile in the development of the phoenix legend. This preliminary discussion will enable us to see the bird and the crocodile as rough equivalents in menstrual myth, in the phoenix legend of self-renewing time, and in the imagery of primitive menstrual rites.

In the preceding chapter I described several wood carvings from New Guinea and New Ireland that depict the phenomenon of menstrual bleeding as the result of an attack by a bird or crocodile. These carved objects correspond not only to the myth of the *chisumi* among the African Luvale, mentioned in chapter 1, but also to myths current among Australian aborigines whose society is one of the most primitive known. Certain totemic creatures such as Native-Companion (a small chicken hawk), Crow, and a reptile with legs, are said to have special significance for aboriginal women because they are linked to the creation of menstrual bleeding.[4] Some tribes explain menstruation via a wound inflicted on one fabled bird by another. For example, Phyllis Kaberry recounts a myth of the Djaru, Lungu, and Wolmeri tribes wherein the monthly flow of blood has its inception when the mythic bird, Native-Companion, inflicts wounds on Crow and little Chicken-Hawk.[5] Similarly, a myth described by Bruno Bettelheim marks the beginning of menstruation from a wound inflicted by a boomerang thrown by a semi-human bird: Junjurilja.[6] The weapon entered the vulvas of his bird-wives, cutting them internally and creating the periodic flow of blood. There are, however, other myths that involve not birds but reptiles. Thus, according to a version of the menstrual myth recounted by the Malngen, the catamenia takes its origin from a wound inflicted by one female reptile on itself and then on another.[7]

From the perspective of myths about menstruation's originating from a self-inflicted wound or a wound inflicted by one animal on another and in the light of the fecund properties early peoples attributed to the resulting flow of blood, it is significant that Horapollo, a Greek gram-

marian living in Egypt during the fourth century A.D. offers a version of
the genesis of the phoenix that differs from the two traditional versions
of renewal through fire or through putrefaction. According to
Horapollo's account, before the old phoenix dies, it inflicts a wound
upon itself, the fluid from which gives rise to the new phoenix.[8] Addi-
tionally, it is striking, when one considers the analogous roles played by
the crocodile and the bird in myths about the genesis of menstruation,
that the phoenix-*benu* and the crocodile both figure in Egyptian representations of childbirth and that, in the development of the phoenix
myth itself, a crocodile has appeared as an analogue to the phoenix. For
instance, in his *Religion of the Ancient Egyptians*, Alfred Wiedemann
reproduces a bas relief depicting the birth of Queen Hatshepsut.[9] Besides four females who kneel in attendance before the infant, there are
four crocodile-headed figures squatting in the middle of the picture who
are presenting the Egyptian sign of life to the child. The suggestion of
the phoenix appears in the presence of a solar deity, Bes, who was lord
of Arabia, "the supposed home of the Sun god and his sacred bird, the
phoenix."[10] Reminding us of the interaction between Egypt and the rest
of Africa, Wiedemann adds that the attire and appearance of the god Bes
suggest that he arose in a Negro country along the southern frontier of
Egypt. The subject of this birth scene is treated in the same way in a
similar bas-relief, found in the temple of Luxor, that represents the birth
of King Amenophis III.[11] A representation depicting the birth of Horus
from the virgin goddess, Isis, also contains an attendant who is a solar
diety. His headdress combines reptilian figures with the solar disc, sign
of the sun god, Ra, while his head is that of a bird—perhaps Ra's
phoenix, or possibly Isis's ibis. The reptilian figures are probably meant
to be crocodiles, since as I observed earlier, Clement of Alexandria, in his
Miscellanies, explains that the Egyptian symbol of the sun rested on
either a ship or a crocodile.[12] Furthermore, as the two amulets discussed
in chapter 1 indicate, the symbol of the sun above the crocodile was
sometimes a phoenix.

In the classical development of the phoenix myth, the crocodile and
the phoenix are also closely related. We have already noted an unmistakable reference to the crocodile in a passage on the phoenix in the
Physiologus of Vienna.[13] In the *Slavonic Enoch*, dated no earlier than the
seventh century, a phoenix and a *chalkedri* (identified by Van den Broek
as a crocodile) are both described as companions of the sun in its path
through the sky.[14] While the Egyptian syncretism of Roman times may
account for the transmission of the combined phoenix and crocodile
motif in the *Slavonic Enoch*, the correspondences between the crocodile
and bird found in menstrual myths of New Guinea and Australia must
be of independent origin. The relatedness of all these parallels to the

Isis. The Birth of Horus. From Harding, Fig. 31. *(By permission of C. G. Jung Foundation. Photo courtesy of General Research and Humanities Division, The New York Public Library, Astor, Lenox, and Tilden Foundations.)*

renewal of time and/or the process of birth suggests that the images reflect a fundamental pattern of the human psyche. Although the combinations of the crocodile and bird that I have mentioned are all symbolic, a distinctive bird-crocodile motif can be found on perfectly functional utensils in British New Guinea where no obvious symbolism attaches to the design, as far as we can determine from the plates and discussion in A. C. Haddon's *Decorative Art of British New Guinea*.[15] The interlaced figures of bird and crocodile may reflect a perceived relationship between the two, but nothing about the use of the objects on which they appear suggests that the designs are intended as anything but decoration. Haddon unfortunately does not explore the possibility of meaning in these decorative figures.

Such is not the case with certain figurines used ceremonially in the course of initiation rites among the Bemba of Northern Rhodesia (the former name of northern Zambia, retained because Audrey Richards uses it in her study of the Bemba) and the Samba of Tanganyika (now Tanzania). An important part of the Bemba *chisungu* involves the modeling of clay animals—a crocodile-like reptile with legs and a guinea fowl—by the older women of the tribe. One of these women reportedly identified the crocodile as "rays of the sun" (*amashindo eya itengo*) and said it was to teach the girl that "the sun was high and she must get on with her work."[16] It was also interpreted as a fertility symbol, as was the clay bird. Strictly speaking the pottery emblems are sacred emblems as they are referred to as *mbusa*, "things handed down."[17] In the course of the female initiation ceremony, the bird design also figured in a guinea fowl drawing that covered the floor of the secluded ceremonial hut and that was dotted with seeds and color. An informant said the guinea fowl was "to remind the girl not to forget her hoe, and that she is to go on giving the people food."[18] Richards concludes, however, that the guinea fowl is not associated merely with agricultural fertility but also with that of the girl's now mature sexuality. A common symbolism is shared among the Bemba, Bisa, Lamba, Lala, Kaonde, and Alungu tribes. The ceremony of a tribe along the bank of the Luanga river, ending three or four months of sequestering following menarche, includes a dance by the young girl on a crocodile design.[19]

In *African Figurines: Their Ceremonial Use in Puberty Rites in Tanganyika*, H. Cory cites a dramatic instance of the ritual use of a wooden bird carving. The novices are led into the bush and made to crawl through a dark tunnel.[20] On returning to the light, they are shown a three-foot woodcarving of a bird while they receive incisions on their arms.[21] Very few tribesmen know the art of making this ceremonial figurine (*ndeghe*), which Cory describes as showing "a certain archaic quality as compared with other figurines. It looks as if the form of the carving was fixed before the didactic possibilities of figurines and their use in initiation rites became popular."[22] The striking thing about this ceremonial bird is that it appears in the initiation ceremony of boys. Cory thinks it may have totemic significance, in which case the figure may have a private meaning for the men of the tribe. Since, however, the final stage of sanctifying a newly crafted bird carving consists of bloodying the beak of the bird, it may be that the figurine has sexual significance. It is possible that the bird seen by the boys at the end of their initiation tunnel symbolizes the female. The bird carving might contain specifically male symbolism, but we have been prepared for such puzzles by the Bird Goddesses with long phallic necks mentioned earlier[23] and by the phoenix poems themselves that, while describing the bird as fulfilling a female function, emphasize the indeterminate nature of the phoenix's sex:

> o fortunatae sortis felixque volucrum,
>   cui de se nasci praestitit ipse deus!
> femina seu [sexu seu] masculus est seu neutrum:
>   felix, quae Veneris foedera nulla colit!
>
> (*Carmen*, 161–64)[24]

[O creature of blessed lot, thou fortunate of the birds, on whom the god has personally conferred birth from thyself! Whether the bird is female or male of sex, or neither, blessed is the Phoenix which cherishes no ties of Venus!]

> . . . God āna wāt,
> Cyning ælmihtig   hū his gecynde biŏ,
> wīfhādes þe weres; . . .
>
> (*The Phoenix*, 355–57)[25]

[. . . God only knows,
The Almighty King,   what his breed may be,
Or male or female; . . .][26]

It may be well, here, to recollect Eliade's idea that "life springs from an over-fullness, from a wholeness."[27]

Thus, just as the androgynous nature of the phoenix does not exclude its female potential, the associations of the bird figure with menstrual myths and female initiation symbolism do not eliminate its potential for use as a masculine sign, if it is such in the instance of the wooden figure from Tanzania.

There are other ways in which bird images appear in female initiation rites apart from their appearance as figurines and related graphic designs. In the Bemba ceremony described by Richards, the bird figures not only in the clay model but also in the ceremonial eating of chickens by all the women, old and young, who take part in the ceremonies.[28] Among the Luvale, the eating of chickens also occurs but is limited to the man who will marry the girl initiate when the ritual of menarche is completed. C. M. N. White writes that the eating of the chicken by the husband "is regarded as symbolic of the marriage: the food provided by the relatives of the girl being the girl herself"[29]

Bird symbolism occasionally appears as a feature of costumes worn in rites marking the first menstrual flow. The initiation ritual of the Nootka Indians of British Columbia provides an example. British Columbia may seem a distant locus for an example, but, as I have already pointed out, there seems to be great similarity among puberal rituals of primitive peoples in areas geographically far removed from one another. The fact may suggest something like universal practice; however, diffusion is not out of the question. Not only have New World archeologists come to speak of ancient Pacific crossings, but Cyrus Gordon makes a case for "transatlantic communication in antiquity" and "the existence of an ancient global ecumene."[30] Franz Boas recounts that during a ceremony which includes ecstatic singing, an element of the bird's actions in both the Old English and the Latin poem, the girl initiate is made to stand between two men dressed in elaborately feathered face and body costumes of a bird called the Thunderbird.[31] Describing the costumes, Boas writes that they "consist each of a large mask, to which a complete dress, set with feathers and having wings, is attached."[32] Meanwhile, eight men from among the singers seize a huge basin, run to the river, fill the basin with water, and pour it on the girl's feet—an action that is repeated several times. When the bathing is complete, a screen painted with the thunderbird design is placed around the girl. An African instance of the use of a bird costume may be cited from the practice of the Caffre of South Africa. The tribe's most elaborate female initiation rituals end when the young girl is led out of her secluded hut by a man wearing the wings of the blue crane on his head.[33] Among the aborigines of northern Australia the girl initiate herself is made to look birdlike. She is decorated with red and white feather down fastened to her skin by her own blood.[34]

Contributing to our sense of the phoenix image as operating within a menstrual context is the striking linguistic evidence concerning blood. First, the phoenix's very name recalls blood. Isidore of Seville's explanation of the derivation of "phoenix" is still found in modern etymological studies. He explains the name of the bird on the basis of the purple color supposed to have been first developed in Phoenicia: "*Phoenix*, Arabiæ avis, dicta, quod colorem Phœniceum habeat."[35] Greek usage, both Homeric and Attic, attests to the blood connotations of phoenix, φοῖνιξ.

The word's origin, of course, is in Phoenicia, the home of the dyers Isidore speaks of, and the word as a substantive or adjective primarily means crimson. But, as Liddell and Scott show, several adjectives and one verb on the φοῖνιξ root have become almost reflex epithets of blood: σμῶδιγγες αἵματι φοινικόεις, "bruises reddened with blood" (*Iliad* 23.717); αἵματι φοινικδεις, "red with blood" (Hesiod, *Scotum Herculis* 194); παρήιον αἵματι φοινόν, "Blood red cheek" (*Iliad* 16.159); αἵματι Ἄρης πόντον φοινίξει "Ares reddens the sea with blood" (Crasulus apud Herodotum, 8.77); and φοινίσσειν "to become blood red" (Nicander, *Therisca*, 238). It is quite possible that the etymology of the bird's name contains the residue of a mythic menstrual association. But the qualification should be made that what is referred to by "blood red" may only be the fabulous bird's color. Herodotus thought the bird was red:

> Another bird also is sacred; it is called the phoenix. I myself have never seen it, but only pictures of it; for the bird comes but seldom into Egypt, once in five hundred years, as the people of Heliopolis say. . . . If the picture truly shows his size and appearance, his plumage is partly golden, but mostly red.[36]

So did Lactantius:

> primo qui color est malis sub sidere Cancri,
> cortice quae croceo Punica grana tegunt;
> qualis inest foliis, quae fert agreste papaver,
> cum pandit vestes Flora rubente solo.
>
> (*Carmen*, 125–28)

> [First, the color which pomegranates have under the sign of the Crab when they cover their seeds with a saffron colored rind; such a hue as is on the petals which the wild poppy flaunts when Flora spreads her skirts over the reddening land.]

These attributions of red color to the bird could, of course, themselves spring from a primitive connection to the origin of menstruation. As the mystery of blood is the experience at the center of female initiation ceremonies, it comes as no surprise to discover that the ceremonies of peoples as far-flung as the Luvale of Africa, the aboringines of the Great Victoria Desert, Australia, the Otabi of the Cape York Peninsula, and the Cheyenne of the Missouri valley include the feature of painting the girl red.[37]

Second, a linguistic detail from the Old English poem which lends support to the idea of the phoenix as a menstrual bird is the reference to his *heorodrēorges hus* (217). In an examination of the range of possible translations for the compound *heorodrēorig*, Karl Wentersdorf points out that *drēorig* is sometimes glossed as "bloody, bloodstained," based on the meaning of *drēor*, "[flowing] blood."[38] While he labels this sense of *drēorig* "archaic," Wentersdorf does observe that, based on this archaic meaning of the second element, *heorodrēorig* could mean "stained with life-blood."[39] Indeed, *heorodrēorig* is clearly a cognate of Old Saxon *herudrôrag* which has the meaning "blood-stained."[40] The context in which the word is used, however, leads Wentersdorf to discount this as a possible translation: "The peaceful bird seated in his nest of aromatic herbs cannot possibly be thought of as covered with gore or even as merely flecked with blood."[41] *Heorodrēorig*, whose first element means "sword," could be classed as a "dead epithet"—one of those phrases from the heroic vocabulary that comes simply to mean "hero" or "bold one" or "warrior" and nothing more. There are several others in the poem, some of which are pointed out by James E. Cross.[42] But the very archaism of the second half of the compound, meaning "[flowing] blood," may point even further back in time to a link to the mythic menstrual bird. If the phoenix can be thought to have anything at all in common with a warrior out of the Germanic heroic tradition, it may be the sense that bravery is required for both war and the birth process. In the light of the quintessential moment of fruitfulness when the sun ignites the phoenix's house—as likely a reference to the bird's body as its nest—thereby bringing on the generation of the new bird, there is something appropriate about the hint of fecund blood. Very likely it is the notion of blood's fecundity that leads William Shakespeare in sonnet 19 to refer to the phoenix (for Shakespeare, a feminine bird) as burning in her blood:

> Devouring time blunt thou the Lyons pawes,
> And make the earth devoure her owne sweet brood,
> Plucke the Keene teeth from the fierce Tygers yawes,
> And burn the long liv'd Phoenix in her blood. . . .[43]

Heat and moisture—here, specifically, blood—are, as we shall see in chapter 3, necessary for the creation of life.[44] Viewing the phoenix in the context of the mythic menstrual bird helps make sense of an otherwise perplexing word.

Third—and I put this forward tentatively—there appears to be something like homonymic punning in the Old English *Phoenix* on *blēdan*, "to bleed," the stem of which, *blēd-*, is a homonym of *blēd*, "blossom" or "fruit." I say "something like" because, since one form is a verb and the other a noun, the words lack the syntactic coincidence that true punning usually has. Nonetheless, the coincidence of the sounds and spelling strikes the ear and eye.[45]

Bathing

Lactantius went his own way in creating the duodecimal overflow of the fountain as well as in introducing the phoenix's ritual bath.

The description of the phoenix's garden at the beginning of the poems has long been admired by scholars. More than seventy years ago Frederick Moorman said of the garden in the Old English poem, "Most of the main features of this landscape are taken from the Latin original, but the English poet has warmed to his subject."[46] No one since has disagreed with that evaluation. One reason may be that, as Lewis's heroine, Jane, reminds us in his novel, *That Hideous Strength,* "Freud said we liked gardens because they were symbols of the female body."[47] That thought made Jane feel uncomfortable. Before she remembered Freud's idea she had been walking through a large garden trying to figure out what garden it reminded her of. Was it the garden from *Peter Rabbit? The Romance of the Rose? Alice?* Paradise? Jane immediately resisted Freud's thought—"but that must be a man's point of view"[48]—although it is not long before she finds herself taking it seriously:

> Presumably gardens meant something different in women's dreams. Or did they? Did men and women both feel interested in the female body and even, though it sounded ridiculous, in almost the same way? A sentence rose to her memory: "The beauty of the female body is the root of joy to the female as well as the male, and it is no accident that the Goddess of Love is older and stronger than the God."[49]

I wonder how seriously Lewis took the idea himself as he wrote this passage in 1943, a decade or so before his essay on the anthropological approach to medieval literature, for it is ironic that my study employs, at least in part, the very method Lewis assails in "The Anthropological Approach" and reveals how the feminine pervades two of the most widely admired garden landscapes in all medieval literature.[50]

Looking more closely at the opening landscape of the two poems, we see that the topography of Lactantius's "locus felix" as well as of the Anglo-Saxon poet's "æþelast londa" offers obvious reflections of the *mons veneris.* First, the Latin, which seems the more elemental for its compactness:

> est locus in primo felix oriente remotus,
> qua patet aeterni maxima porta poli

nec tamen aestivos hiemisve propinquus ad ortus,
   sed qua Sol verno fundit ab axe diem.
illic planities tractus diffundit apertos,
   nec tumulus crescit nec cava vallis hiat;
sed nostros montes, quorum iuga celsa putantur,
   per bis sex ulnas eminet ille locus.
hic Solis nemus est et consitus arbore multa
   lucus, perpetuae frondis honore virens.

(1–10)

sed fons in medio [est], quem "vivum" nomine dicunt,
   perspicuus, lenis, dulcibus uber aquis,
qui semel erumpens per singula tempora mensum
   duodecies undis inrigat omne nemus.
hic genus arboreum procero stipite surgens
   non lapsura solo mitia poma gerit.
hoc nemus, hos lucos avis incolit unica Phoenix

(25–31)

[In the farthest East, where opens the mighty portal of the
eternal skies, there lies a spot, blessed, sequestered; yet not near
the summer or the winter risings, but where the Sun sheds the
light from his vernal chariot. There a plain spreads its vast
reaches, not a knoll rises nor a hallow vale opens; but that place
o'ertops by twice six ells our mountains, and their summits are
deemed lofty.

   Here is the grove of the Sun, a holy wood thickly planted with
trees, green with the glory of never-failing foliage.]

[... Yet in the midst of the grove there is a spring, clear,
tranquil, rich in sweet waters, which men call the "Fountain of
Life."

   Once in the course of each month it wells forth and bathes all
the grove twelve times with its waters. Here a variety of tree,
rising with lofty trunk, bears mellow fruit not destined to fall to
earth.]

The corresponding description in the Old English poem is by comparison prolix, owing to its author's habit of redundancy and his fre-
quent addition of Christian references. Nonetheless, the image of the
female genitalia does come through, even if diffusely:

Þæt is wynsum wong,   wealdas grēne,
rūme under roderum. . . .

(13–14)

            . . . Is þæt æþele lond
blōstmum geblōwen.   Beorgas þǣr ne muntas

steape ne stondað,   ne stanclifu
heah hlifiað,[51]   swa her mid us.

(20–23)

                . . . ne þær hleonað oo
unsmeþes wiht,   ac se æþele feld
wrīdað under wolcnum,   wynnum geblōwen.
Is þæt torhte lond,   twelfum herra,
folde fæðmrimes,   swa ūs gefreogum gleawe
witgan þurh wisdom   on gewritum cyþað,
þonne ænig þara beorga   þe her beorhte mid ūs
hea hlifiað   under heofontunglum.
Smylte is se sigewong;   sunbearo līxeð,
wuduholt wynlic,   wæstmas ne dreosað,
beorhte blede,   ac þa beamas a
grene stondað,   swa him God bibead.

(25–36)

                . . . Foldan leccaþ
wæter wynsumu   of þæs wuda midle;
þa mōnþa gehwam   of þære moldan tyrf
brimcald brecað,   bearo ealne geondfarað
þragum þrymlice.   Is þæt þeodnes gebod,
þætte twelf sīþum   þæt tīrfæste
long geondlace   laguflōda wynn.

(64–70)

[The plain is winsome,   the woods are green,
Widespread under heaven. . . .

                . . . The lovely land
Is rich with blossoms.   No mountains rise,
No lofty hills,   as here with us.

Naught rough or rugged;   but the pleasant plain
Basks under heaven   laden with bloom.
        Twelve cubits higher   is that lovely land,
As learned writers   in their books relate,
Than any of these hills   that here in splendour
Tower on high   under heavenly stars.
Serene that country,   sunny groves gleaming;
Winsome the woodlands;   fruits never fail
Or shining blossoms.   As God gave bidding.

        From the midst of the wood   a winsome water
Each month breaks out   from the turf of earth,
Cold as the sea-stream,   coursing sweetly
Through all the grove.   By the bidding of God
The flood streams forth   through the glorious land
Twelve times yearly. . . .]

The parallels between the *mons veneris* and the terrain described in these two passages clearly invite comment: the pleasant plain placed on the highest of hills corresponds to the *labia majora* by the raised *mons;* Lactantius's trees and undying fronds and the Anglo-Saxon poet's blossoms suggest pubic hair; the monthly irrigation, the catamenia; the renewing death of the phoenix who inhabits the garden, *la petite mort;* and so forth.

In the notes to her edition of the *Carmen,* Mary C. Fitzpatrick, almost as if uneasy about her conclusion, observes of the appearance of the number twelve in the description of the fountain: "This number is very common in the closing chapters of the *Apocalypse,* and it seems as though we must accept the idea that it is from here that Lactantius takes it, especially when we recall that here we have its first use in any connection with the Phoenix legend."[52] Apocalypse 22:1–2 is especially striking:

> And he shewed me a pure river of water of life, clear as crystal, proceeding out of the throne of God and of the Lamb. In the midst of the street of it, and on either side of the river, was there the tree of life, which bore twelve manner of fruits, and yielded her fruit every month.[53]

Striking though the use of the number twelve is in this passage, it still leaves us with unanswered questions: why should the fountain rather than the tree be linked to the number twelve? And why should a bird bathe in it? Why, in fact, should a phoenix be in the garden at all? Blake concludes, about this last question, that we cannot say, although there are similarities between the myth of the phoenix and the idea of the *locus amoenus.*[54] Added to these questions is that of whether Lactantius had yet become a Christian when he wrote the *Carmen*—a matter that would affect our opinion of the likely influence of the Apocalypse on his description of the phoenix's fountion. Arturo Graf, for one, believes that Lactantius's opening garden description does not depict a scriptural garden, but rather a garden from another tradition, the Wood of the Sun.[55]

These puzzling innovations are, it seems to me, of a piece with others that critics have wondered about: the association of the phoenix with the garden, which Lactantius carries out in detail for the first time, the introduction of the flight of the phoenix to Syria and its death there in a palm tree, and his treatment of the worm.[56] By showing how these matters are interconnected within the framework of gynecological imagery, this study can, it seems to me, begin to offer some consistent answers to these questions.

For now, let us pause over the question of bathing in the fountain. Ceremonial bathing brings us to the second element of menarche ritual that may be reflected in the Menstrual Sequence contained in the poems. Ceremonial puberal ablutions are performed by many primitive peoples in many parts of the world: the Bakairi of Brazil, the Shuswap of British Columbia, the Guari of India, the Veddas of Ceylon, the Algonquin of North America, among others.[57] Ferdinand von Reitzenstein, in an early study of African nuptial and puberal rites, concludes that ceremonial ablutions had two purposes: the obvious one of cleansing and the more mysterious one of promoting fertility.[58] Imagined as an independent entity, the womb was believed to swallow the seeds of life from the watery element, itself believed to have an influence on sexual maturity. Eliade, speaking more generally about water and the seeds of things, observes that the effect of immersion in water during initiation rituals is to confer new birth.[59] "Water, moon, and woman," he argues, form an "orbit of fertility," one that is mirrored in the carved spirals of Paleolithic art which, when inscribed on female figures, unite "all these centers of life and fertility."[60] Ploss and Bartels report that the Veddas perform an initiation ceremony for menstruating girls which includes ten days of daily ritual ablutions culminating in a final ceremonial bath wherein rubbing with tumeric and oil is added to the usual washing.[61] The coming of menarche continues to be celebrated in modern-day Ceylon where Brahmins practice a ceremony that incorporates the wish for a productive life with a milk bath. Long hours of immersion regardless of the weather characterize the custom of the Bawenda of the North Transvaal observed by Bauster in the late nineteenth century.[62] The Bawenda lead the girls to be initiated to the riverside as do the Basuto in a ceremony called *pollo* and the Bemba in their *chisungu*. Riverside initiation is, in fact, by and large the rule, and was a feature of the Thunderbird ceremony described by Boas. (In that case, however, water is taken from the river to the girl.) Thus, when the phoenix bathes in the cold welling waters of the fountain as the sun rises in the east, we see an analogue to the bathing motif in rituals celebrating menarche.

Seclusion

The third feature wherein primitive rite and poem appear to overlap is the motif of seclusion. Seclusion is accomplished in the ritual as well as in the poems in two ways: by simple withdrawal and by withdrawal to a height. We will consider the simple retreat first. The place in which the phoenix bathes is remote:

> Hæbbe ic gefrugnen   þætte is feor heonan
> ēastdǣlum on   æþelast londa
> fīrum gefrǣge. . . .
>
> (*The Phoenix*, 1–3)

[Lo! I have learned   of the loveliest of lands
Far to the eastward,   famous among men.]

Est locus in primo felix oriente remotus.

(*Carmen*, 1)

[In the farthest East . . . there lies a spot, blessed, sequestered. . . .]

Amplifying the idea of remoteness in the Old English poem is the
Christianizing addition that God set this place apart from the sinful (3–
6). The usual view of the phoenix's remote garden in the east, as described in the Old English poem, is that it represents the earthly paradise,[63] and Lactantius's *Solis nemus*, whether viewed by the critics as
pagan or Christian, is often enough said to share characteristics with the
Garden of Eden.[64] It is clear that the garden's inaccessibility and its
position on a mountain give it two features of the realm of the Other-
world, analyzed by Howard Rollin Patch, as found in Christian and non-
Christian descriptions alike.[65] While, however, these parallels are plain
to see, they do not provide a key to the origin of the phoenix's garden
that promises to unlock the answer to the question of the bird's presence
there. Such a key may be provided by the isolation of the female initiate
during the ceremony that marks her coming of age.

Both Latin and English poets emphasize the solitary nature of the
bird's way of life.

Ðone wudu weardaþ   wundrum fæger
fugel feþrum strong,   sē is fenix hāten.
Þǣr se ānhaga[66]   eard bihealdeþ,
dēormōd drohtað; . . . .

(*The Phoenix*, 85–88)

[In that woodland dwelleth,   most wondrous fair
And strong of wing,   a fowl called Phoenix;
There dauntless-hearted   he has his home,
His lonely lodging. . . .]

hoc nemus, hos lucos avis incolit unica Phoenix:
unica sed vivit morte refecta sua.

(*Carmen*, 31–32)

[This grove, these woods, a unique bird, inhabits, the Phoenix;
but though sole of her kind, she lives born anew of her own
death.]

Seclusion is one of the common denominators of ceremonies of initiation
and is achieved through various means: by taking the girls into a jungle,

a woodland, or, at least, an area with trees at some distance from the community's huts, and by using props or special dwellings which hide. R. M. and C. H. Berndt's summary of this "pervasive theme" (as they call it) of puberal rites among the aborigines of Australia, for instance, would offer a clear statement of the phoenix's social and spatial isolation from the "real world" as it follows its cycle of life in the paradisial garden: "A rite, or series of rites, marks the onset of puberty . . . usually it entails separation from the round of everyday life, a social withdrawal, a movement away from the main camp."[67] There are, indeed, some ceremonies that enhance the sense of isolation by making actual screening or enclosure a part of the ceremony. Such is the case among the Bemba described by Richards:

> The company rushed out with a good deal of laughter and talking to a small *mufungo* tree that stood on the village garden mounds. The two girls trailed behind still covered by blankets, pushed and shoved along by the younger helpers. There were no men present and young children were warned off by excited screams. Nangoshye [a kind of novice mistress] . . . made the girls crouch against the stem of the tree while the woman built a sort of windscreen of branches round them. This was described as "hiding the girls."[68]

This passage describes one of the rare occasions when the girl initiates, participating in daylight ceremonies, were permitted outside of a darkened hut—and even then they cover themselves with blankets and are ritually hidden by tree branches. When the girls are first brought to the hut they crawl on all fours, under blankets, while the following tunnel song is sung:

> Tuingile shijani?
> Tuingile mipempe;
> Nga bakolwe.
>
> [How are we going in?
> We are going in as through a
>   tunnel into a dark place.
> We are going in like monkeys.][69]

One of the immediate interpretations of the song offered by an older female participant was, "We have to go through dark and difficult places before we get wisdom"—presumably the wisdom of a new mode of being.[70] The detail of building the windscreen of branches must, I think, be a parallel to what Boas and Gilbert M. Sproat witnessed in the enclosure of girl initiates in British Columbia by means of a screen painted with the thunderbird design.[71] Among the Arapesh and natives of Vaté Island (one of the New Hebrides), sequestering girls who menstruate for the first time in special huts seems to accomplish the same end.[72] The mode of seclusion of Luvale girls in Zambia, observed by White in the 1950s, is almost a paradigm of the phoenix's behavior as it passes the predawn hours in the garden and fountain area and the hours of day aloft in its tree. White writes, "During the rite the girl lives in a special hut at nights, and by day spends her time away from the village mainly at a tree."[73] Young Shuswap leave their communities at menarche and go to special huts in the hills.[74] The Bemba ceremony takes place in the woodlands as does that of the Chaga who take their female initiates to "a shrubby wilderness."[75] Such is the terrain of the phoenix poems. The plain on the high hill in the Old English poem is called *weald* (13, "forest," "wood"), *feld* (26, "open land"), *wuduholt* (34, "forest"), *wuda* (65, "wood"), and suchlike, and the phoenix itself, *bearwes bigenga* (148, "dweller of the woods"). The bird in the Latin poem lives in a grove (9, "arbore").

Eliade's interpretation of the characteristic seclusion common to the initiation ceremonies is that it represents "a symbolism which is at once that of the beyond, hence, of death, and that of the darkness of gestation in the mother's womb."[76] Thus, the darkened tunnel of the young Bemba women, the screen of the Nootka girls, the huts of the Zambian and Shuswap initiates, and the phoenix's forest or grove may be thought of as symbolizing the idea that before entering upon a new, sanctified existence, the neophyte must die to the profane and infantile. The aborigines of the Great Victoria Desert, Australia, enhance the suggestion of the life and death motif in the girl's seclusion by painting her with white clay and red ochre.[77] In the poems, the phoenix's withdrawal is placed in a cosmological frame through the bird's close association with the aurora, bringer of day from night.

Not only is the bird's home secluded and remote, it is higher than any mountains known, a detail which brings us to the second mode of withdrawal in the poems and in female initiation rites: the assumption of a position above ground. That the phoenix's home is far to the east raises it to a great height:

> Is þæt torhte lond,   twelfum hērra
> folde fæðmrīmes,   swā ūs gefreogum glēawe
> wītgan þurh wīsdōm   on gewritum cȳþað,
> þonne ǣnig þāra beorga   þe hēr beorhte mid ūs
> hēa hlīfiað   under heofontunglum.
>
> (*The Phoenix*, 28–32)

> [Twelve cubits higher   is that lovely land,
> As learned writers   in their books relate,

Than any of these hills   that here in splendour
Tower on high   under heavenly stars.]

sed nostros montes, quorum iuga celsa putantur,
    per bis sex ulna imminet ille locus.

(Carmen, 7–8)

[. . . but that place o'ertops by twice six ells our mountains, and their summits are deemed lofty.]

Moreover, when, after its ritual bath, the phoenix flies to a perch on a lofty tree (*Carmen*, 39–40; *The Phoenix*, 111–12), it assumes a position that is more distant still. By flying aloft to a tree, the phoenix places itself in a position above ground that is the formal pose, in many parts of the world, imposed upon girls participating in puberal rituals. The prohibition "not to touch the ground" was found by Sir James Frazer to be a general "rule" of female initiations.[78] In Loango, Africa, he observed that "girls at puberty are confined in separate huts, and they may not touch the ground with any part of their bare body."[79] Among several tribes of the plateau west of Lake Tanganyika as well as the Nyanja-speaking tribes of Central Angoniland the prohibition manifested itself in the curious procedure of transporting the female initiate on the back of the old woman charged with directing the puberal ceremonies.[80] Similarly, C. Velten reports of Swahili female initiates that they are carried on the backs of older women.[81] Food prohibitions, often limiting the young girl to water only accompany the removal to a level above ground and may be reflected in the Latin and Old English poems by the phoenix's drinking water at the overflowing fountain immediately before flying up to the tree.

The removal of the female initiate to a level above ground during her initiation is characteristic of ceremonies outside Africa as well. Again, the removal is accompanied by special diet, usually little more than water. Sproat reports of the Nootka Indians of Vancouver, for example, that, "On reaching puberty, young women . . . are placed in the sort of gallery already described in every house . . . . In this cage they remain for several days. Water is given to them, but no food."[82] It should be recalled that while in the cage the girl is surrounded by pictures of a mythical bird (the "thunderbird"). Similarly, the Kolosh Indians of Alaska confine girls to cages (sometimes huts) at the first sign of puberty. It is notable that as with the confinement of the Nootka women, the bird motif appears along with the raised enclosure. Frazer observes that the girl "had to drink out of the wing-bone of a white-headed eagle."[83] The most dramatic example of seclusion above ground that I have encountered is that cited by Frazer of girls in New Ireland confined for as long as five years in cages suspended from the ceilings of small houses known as *bucks*. The cages themselves, which one observer likened to hencoops,[84] were constructed from the leaves of a local tree, the pandanus, and were so small that the girls could only sit or lie down in a bent position. Because the doors of the *buck* were always kept closed, the cages containing the girls were almost completely dark. It goes without saying that the combination of the dark and the crouched position of the girls offers a graphic representation of a return to their beginning in the womb.[85]

More broadly, the prohibition against touching ground, found in so many ceremonies of female initiation, suggests that the initiate is thought of as moving toward a more spiritual mode of being that is conditioned by the revelations of the sexual and the sacred. Indeed, as Eliade has argued, for the primitive "the mystery of giving birth—that is, the woman's discovery that she is creative upon the plane of life— amounts to a religious experience."[86] It is primarily her role as creatress for which the girl is prepared by the process of initiation that includes instruction in the secrets of sexuality. Birth is also the climactic moment of the poems toward which the actions of the phoenix lead. A position above ground is a natural representation of the idea of transcendence, and, according to Hutton Webster, even the seclusion and abstinence from food are connected "with a primitive effort to assimilate the novice to the condition of spirits."[87] The bird, naturally endowed with the ability to fly above the universe, is peculiarly fitted to embody transcendence:

> tollitur ac summo considit in arboris altae
> vertice, quae totum despicit una nemus,
> et conversa novos Phoebi nascentis ad ortus
> expectat radios at iubar exoriens.
>
> (*Carmen*, 39–42)

[She soars, and lights on the topmost part of a lofty tree which is the only one that looks down on the whole grove; and turned toward the risings of new-born Phoebus, she awaits his rays and the growing light.]

> Siþþan hine sylfne   æfter sundplegan
> hēahmōd hefeð   on hēanne bēam,
> þonan ȳþast mæg   on ēastwegum
> sīð bihealdan   hwonne swegles tapur,
> ofer holmþræce   hædre blīce
> lēohtes lēoma.
>
> (*The Phoenix*, 111–16)

[Thereafter the proud one   after his water-play
Takes his flight   to a lofty tree

> Whence most easily   o'er the eastern ways
> He beholds the course   of the heavenly taper
> Brightly shining   over the tossing sea,
> A blaze of light.]

In light of the relationship that scholars have seen between seclusion and the idea of being reborn to a new status in puberal initiations—male as well as female[88]—it is remarkable that the stated motive for the phoenix's flight upward in both poems is that it may thereby more easily watch the rising sun as it appears in the east. Eliade's lucid analysis of the meaning of seclusion in initiation makes the object of the phoenix's attention seem particularly apt in this ritual context: "It is necessary to abolish the work of Time, and to reenter the auroral instant prior to the Creation: on the human plane this amounts to saying that one must return to the 'blank page' of existence, the absolute commencement when nothing had yet been defiled."[89] It is, perhaps, paradoxical that the phoenix should watch for dawn at all, for it lives in a timeless world where, as the Old English poet writes, "onwended ne bið" (83, "change never comes"), and the phoenix itself is "wlitigfæst" (105, "changeless in beauty"). In terms of Eliade's " 'blank page' of existence, the absolute commencement," the phoenix makes the quintessential initiate, frozen in the perfection of the auroral instant (for a thousand years, anyway). In a constant cycle of perchings upon its tree, the bird continually waits in expectation of the aurora—that is, the Creation, an analogue of its re-creation. It is as if before becoming a new phoenix, the first phoenix must relive the cosmology. When the bird is ready to change—when it is ready to give birth to itself and renew its "changelessness"—it must leave the perfect changeless world and temporarily enter the waste or the world as we know it, another scene of seclusion that we will consider in a subsequent chapter.

I have left for last the question of what finally triggers the phoenix's release from the isolation of the *weald* or *arbor*. Bearing in mind that Lactantius developed the "whole story of the flight of the phoenix to Syria and its death there in a palm tree,"[90] I think there is reason to believe that he had in mind the kind of practices surrounding feminine rituals that I have been discussing. In this light, therefore, I reason that the end of the menstrual frame of time is what ends the phoenix's seclusion or, to put it another way, conception ends it. Margaret Mead once defined menstruation as a time when "the body prepares itself tirelessly for the impregnation that may come but does not."[91] The poems, as I read them, describe the cycle of the bird's life and present it at the moment when impregnation by the sun is, as it were, a success, that once in a thousand years. The cycle thus broken, the phoenix moves out of the changeless, menstrual frame of time. (We will turn to a detailed consideration of the sun's generative role in the following chapter dealing with the Conception Sequence.)

Those scholars who have studied the allegorical meaning of *The Phoenix* interpret the bird's movement out of the garden of that poem in a variety of related ways. Daniel Calder, for instance, takes the view that the "journey out of paradise symbolizes the exile of the sinful from God's grace,"[92] an interpretation close to a brief one offered in the homiletic second half of the Old English poem itself; the latter explains how the phoenix signifies Adam and Eve and how the first human couple had to abandon Eden and wander in a long journey of earthly existence (440). One of the most specialized readings is John Bugge's. Bugge argues that the phoenix's life corresponds to the spiritual life of the monk and that we must see "þisses fugles gefǣr (426b) to *middangeard* as a type of monastic exile: reaching Syria (notably, along with Egypt, the site of the eremetical life of the desert fathers), it engages in unmistakably anchoritic conduct."[93] With these and other similar allegorical approaches to the Old English text, I have no quarrel; each testifies to the richness and flexibility of the allegory, whose technique Calder aptly describes as "kaleidoscopic" in its "constantly shifting, fading, and merging perspectives."[94] In chapter 5, I put forth yet another possible allegorical reading that emerges as a result of my findings. What is essential, in my view, is that all the possible readings be thought of as revalorizations of a pagan movement inherited from Lactantius who, as Calder points out in another context, "at no time refers to a system of Christian theology" even if the poem has been subjected to such inquiry.[95]

Trees

The tree in the landscape of the phoenix poems, touched on in our consideration of seclusion above ground, takes us to the fourth and last element common to the Menstrual Sequence and the primitive celebrations of menarche. As was demonstrated in the previous discussion, the position above ground symbolizes transcendence, the idea that the initiate as well as the bird is about to be reborn to a new and more spiritual mode of being. I would like to begin this examination of the tree as a common element in female initiation ritual and the phoenix poems by developing further the relationship between transcendence and height, here specifically embodied in the tree image.

The phoenix's ascent to a high tree, at lines 39–40 of the *Carmen* and lines 111–12 of *The Phoenix*, has its parallel in the ritual climbing of trees that characterizes female initiation ceremonies in many primitive societies of Africa, Australia, and North America. Among the Cewa of the Dowa district of Nyasaland, described by A. G. O. Hodgson, young girls are made to climb trees on the first day of the ceremonies and are then carried into the village on the backs of older women.[96] In the meanings attributed to such climbs the natives demonstrate considerable variety. The Shuswap of British Columbia, for instance, believe the climb will make the girl strong.[97] The Bemba of Rhodesia, on the other hand, consider the climb a token of the "impossible things" a girl must learn to do: i.e., fetch firewood, ignore a husband's adultery.[98] Such explanations are pragmatic and reveal modern primitives' forgetfulness of the spiritual significance of some of their customs. Even in more civilized societies many people would be hard pressed to explain the meaning of some of their own religious rituals.

We may get a sense of the spiritual meaning of the female initiate's climbing a tree—and by extension, of the phoenix's climb—by studying another ritual ascent: that of the shaman. If, as Frazer observes, "the uncleanness . . . of girls at puberty and the sanctity of holy men . . . are only different manifestations of the same mysterious energy,"[99] there may be parallels between the climbs that are aspects of the ritual initiation of both.

In "The Yearning for Paradise in Primitive Tradition," Eliade examines the shaman's ability to reestablish communications between Heaven and Earth, which broke down, according to early Australian, African, Southeast Asian, and Oceanic myths, after a catastrophe similar to the Fall.[100] In the primordial time, "men could ascend to Heaven by climbing a mountain, a tree, a vine, or a ladder or have themselves carried there by birds."[101] The shaman's initiation ceremony enables the initiate to accomplish the ascent to Heaven, as in that paradisial period, through the symbolic climb of a tree (or upright pole). However, the recovery of the unity between Heaven and Earth that existed in the mythical days of the lost paradise, thus achieved by the shaman, is only partial. Eliade explains that he "ascends to Heaven 'in spirit,' no longer *in concreto* as did primordial man. He does not abrogate death."[102] So, too, the immortality achieved by the two other ascenders of the tree, the female initiate and the phoenix, is not that of the true primordial paradise. The woman, as creatress, will not achieve immortality in her own person but through her offspring; likewise, the phoenix will achieve a qualified immortality—post-mortem, through its offspring, every thousand years.[103]

Once initiated, the shaman has another way of temporarily bridging the gap between Heaven and Earth and reentering the initial state of humanity: that is, through the ecstatic trance. Like the girl who has arrived at first menstruation, the shaman in the state of trance is believed by the primitive to have sacred powers. Even more, the shaman in the state of ecstasy resembles the fabulous avian tree climber. While he is entranced, the shaman's spirit is said to fly through the air,[104] and according to observers he makes many birdlike sounds. Wencelas Sieroszewski writes of the Yakutsk shamans:

> Tout à coup retentit, on ne sait où, un cri aigu. . . . tantôt en haut, tantôt en bas, tantôt devant, tantôt derrière le chamane. . . . on croirait entendre le cri plaintif du vanneau, mêlé au croassement d'un faucon qu'interrompt le sifflement de la bécasse: c'est le chamane qui crie ainsi en variant les intonations de sa voix. . . . on entend le croassement des aigles auquel se mêlent les plaintes des vanneaux, les cris perçants des bécasses et le refrain des coucous.[105]

> [Suddenly a sharp cry resounds from one knows not where. . . . sometimes from above, sometimes from below, sometimes in front of, sometimes behind the shaman. . . . One seems to hear the plaintive call of the lapwing mingled with the croaking of a falcon interrupted by the whistle of the woodchuck: all that is the voice of the shaman, varying the intonations of his voice. . . . one hears the screaming of eagles mingled with the plaints of the lapwing, the sharp cries of the woodchuck and the refrain of the cuckoo.]

The bird sounds described in the passage make clear that the shaman's mystical transcendence of the fallen, human condition is associated with avian qualities. Certainly the bird's power to defy gravity and raise itself above the earth makes it an ideal symbol of the spiritual. The eighth-century Anglo-Saxon poet of *The Phoenix* thought so. In his allegorical reading of the poem's symbols in the second half of the poem, a subject we will examine closely in chapter 5, he interprets the phoenix as a symbol of the good Christian who reaches the heavenly kingdom.

But to return to the tree. From the perspective of this image as a shared element in the Menstrual Sequence of the phoenix poems and female initiation ritual, the tree is not merely, to borrow a phrase from the Old English poet, to be thought of as

> . . . se hēa bēam   in þām hālge nū
> wīc weardiað. . . .
>
> (447–48)

> [. . . the high tree in which the holy
> Have their habitation. . . .]

Trees, like rivers and springs, are associated with reproduction in primitive belief,[106] and so it is not surprising to discover that special trees called "women's trees" are used in the ceremonies to ensure fertility.[107] The Bemba have their *mwenge, mufungu,* and *musuku;* the Chaga, the *mringonu;* the Luvale, the *muulya, musole,* and *munjongolo* trees; and the Masai, the doom palm.[108] It is difficult to determine from the ceremonial events that occur at trees to what extent they symbolize the hoped-for fertility of the girl herself or to what degree the fertility may be linked with the gardens it will be her responsibility to cultivate for her family's food. To be sure, human and agricultural fertility are perceived as analogous and, therefore, distinctions are blurred. There are actions that occur at "women's trees" in the Bemba ceremony which clearly mime gardening: ground is churned up, seeds sown, and roots watered.[109] On the other hand, some ritual acts clearly are linked to the fertility of the girl herself. R. Devers, for instance, recounts of ceremonies in Mutshtoha, Africa, that girls are made to lie for a time in front of a *mbudi* tree before their period of seclusion,[110] and O. F. Raum describes the Chaga's use of the *mringonu* in an instructional allegory of fetal anatomy.[111] The initiate is given a lesson with the branch of the tree as a prop. Raum explains, "Each lesson on a ring begins with: 'Your grandfather notched you in your mother's womb and such and such an organ grew.' With the longitudinal strips referring to sinews, bones and veins, the observation is: 'Your grandfather stretched you in your mother's womb and such and such a part came into being.'"[112] Some ceremonies seem to attempt an identification of the girl with the tree itself and hence with its fertility: Kenyan initiates decorate their hair with leaves of the doom palm;[113] Luvale women live in initiation huts made of women's trees;[114] and Haida Indian girls (of Queen Charlotte Islands) wear cloaks of cedar bark for several months.[115]

We may infer from the general description of trees in the Menstrual Sequences of the Latin and Old English poems that the tree to which the phoenix flies is fertile. In the Latin poem, the tall tree overtopping the grove where the phoenix perches is probably that described eight lines earlier this way by Lactantius:

> hic genus arboreum procero stipite surgens
> non lapsura solo mitia poma gerit.
>
> (29–30)

> [Here a variety of tree, rising with lofty trunk, bears mellow fruit not destined to fall to earth.]

What the Anglo-Saxon poet says of all trees in the phoenix's garden must also apply to the lofty one from which the phoenix watches the sunrise:

> . . . ac þær wrætlīce
> on þām trēowum symle   telgan gehladene,
> ofett ednīwe   in ealle tīd.
>
> (75–77)

[But in every season   on all the trees
The boughs bear their burden   of fruit anew.]

It is not until the post-menstrual section of the poem, after the phoenix journeys to Syria to another wooded, secret place, that a name is
given to the lofty tree on which the bird alights:

```
              æghwylc     wille
wesan þegn ond þēow        þēodne mǣrum
oþþæt hȳ gesēcað        Syrwara lond
corðra mǣste.      Him se clǣna þǣr
oðscūfeð scearplīce        þæt hē in scade weardað
on wudubearwe      wēste stōwe
biholene ond bihȳdde        hæleþa monegum.
Ðǣr hē hēanne bēam        on holtwuda
wunað ond weardað        wyrtum fæstne
under heofumhrōfe,        þone hātað men
fenix on foldan      of þæs fugles noman.
```
(The Phoenix, 164–74)

[And so he seeks out   the Syrian land
With a lordly following.   There the pure fowl
Suddenly leaves them,   lodging in shadow
In a woodland covert,   a secret spot
Sequestered and hidden   from the hosts of men.
     There he takes lodging   in a lofty tree
Fast by its roots   in the forest-wood
Under heaven's roof.   The race of men
Call the tree Phoenix   from the name of the fowl.]

dirigit in Syriam celeres longaeva volatus,
   Phoenices nomen cui dedit ipsa vetus,
secretosque petit deserta per avia lucos,
   sicubi per saltus silva remota latet.
tum legit aerio sublimem vertice palmam,
   quae Graium phoenix ex ave nomen habet.
(Carmen, 65–70)

[The aged bird directs her swift flight to Syria, upon which the
original Phoenix bestowed the name Phoenicia. Along the track-
less wastes she seeks secluded groves, wheresoever through the
glens a far-off wood lies hidden. Next she chooses a palm with
top towering high in air, a tree which derives its Greek name
"phoenix" from the bird.]

Unlike Lactantius who draws attention to the fact that in Greek the same
word is used to mean, "phoenix," "Phoenician," and "palm" the Anglo-
Saxon poet simply leaves the matter at linking the tree's name to the

bird. Ovid says nothing at all about etymology, but calls the tree in which the phoenix builds its nest in preparation for renewing itself a palm: *ilicet in ramis tremulaeque cacumino palmae / unguibus et puro nidum sibi construit ore* (*Metam.* 15, 396–97).[116] Liddell and Scott indicate that the word φοῖνιξ refers, among other things, not only to the fabulous bird phoenix, but to two different types of palm tree: the date palm *(Phoenix dactylifera)* and the dwarf palm *(Chamaerops humilis)*. A curious fact bears witness to how strangely these matters are interwoven: it happens that the two kinds of palm are linked botanically as well as linguistically. E. J. H. Corner, a tropical botanist at the University of Cambridge, explains that on the basis of structural similarities between the species *phoenix* and the genus *chamaerops*, it can be assumed that the two palms evolved from a common ancestor.[117] When we turn from the Greek to the Egyptian word for palm the connections are equally striking: *benu*, the name of the Egyptian prototype of the phoenix, is a word which in Egyptian means "palm tree" as well as the bird, just as φοῖνιξ does in Greek.[118]

Palm iconography and mythology are equally illuminating as palm etymology and botany. About the association of phoenix and palm in art Van den Broek comments, "In early Christian art the phoenix was often shown on a palm tree, but these are always representations of the heavenly Paradise, both the phoenix and the palm being symbols of the triumph of Life Over Death, and have nothing to do with a phoenix on the point of renewing its life, as in Lactantius and Ovid. The latter is first encountered in illustrated medieval books."[119] Although the phoenix may not be linked in art to the palm until the Middle Ages, a link is made between the birth process and the palm in ancient Greece and Rome. It is known that Greek women, believing the sign of victory would help them bear the pains of childbirth, held twigs of palm trees in their hands.[120] Similarly, on a Roman vase depicting the birth of Apollo, Leto is shown clasping a palm tree while imploring the aid of the Dii Nixi, goddesses of childbirth.[121] The qualification should, however, be made that in ancient Rome the usefulness of the palm in gynecological procedures was not limited to delivery. Pliny says, for example, that it may be used in controlling the menses:

> The palm . . . found in Egypt, is very highly esteemed. It has no stone in its dates, as other date-palms have. Taken in dry wine it checks . . . excessive menstruation. . . .[122]

Thus the lofty tree, unnamed in the menstrual sections of both the Latin and Old English poems, could be a palm. Indeed, although, the Anglo-Saxon poet does not identify the tree as *Fenix* until line 174, in the Birth

Sequence, he describes it the same way in both parts of the poem: *heanne beam* (112, 171, "lofty tree"), and this seems to correspond to Lactantius's *arboris altae* (39, "tall tree"). Such descriptions could accurately be applied to the phoenix palm. Corner describes it as "the tallest" of the palms, reaching "over eighty feet high."[123] Moreover, in terms of the time the phoenix spends in its thousand-year cycle of daily perchings on the lofty tree, the phoenix palm is appropriate: it can live for more than a century.[124]

The Menstrual Sequence's cycle of ceaselessly repeated actions is broken when the generative light of the sun brings change to the changeless landscape. Bathed in the sun's warm light, the singing phoenix opens the Conception Sequence.

3

THE CONCEPTION SEQUENCE

Song and the sun—two elements that appear in the Old English poem (120–47) as well as in the Latin *Carmen* (43–54)—may be thought of as belonging to a Conception Sequence. For the first time in the phoenix poems, early scientific theories of generation are felt to draw into the imagery as much as, if not more than, ritual. That should come as no surprise, for the sun that Lactantius and the Anglo-Saxon poet depict as so potent in its action on the phoenix commanded the attention of both primitive peoples and early scientists. Each recognized the sun as primary in the development of life.

Song

First let us consider the role played by song. The phoenix greets the rising sun with song from the tree on which it sits after a bath in the fountain's water. Lactantius and the Anglo-Saxon poet both describe the singing as uniquely beautiful. The English poem gives the subject of the song's special nature twelve lines:

> wrixleð wōðcræfte,   wundorlīcor
> beorhtan reorde   þonne ǣfre byre monnes
> hȳrde under heofonum,   siþþan Hēahcyning,
> wuldres Wyrhta   woruld staþelode,
> heofon ond eorþan.   Biþ þæs hlēoðres swēg
> eallum songcræftum   swētra ond wlitigra
> ond wynsumra   wrenca gehwylcum;
> ne magon þām breahtme   bȳman ne hornas
> ne hearpan hlyn,   ne hæleþa stefn
> ǣnges on eorþan   ne organan,
> swēglēoþres geswin   ne swanes feðre
> ne ǣnig þāra drēama   þe Dryhten gescōp
> gumum tō glīwe   in þās gēomran woruld.

(127–39)

> [More wondrous music   than ever child of man
> Heard under heaven   since the High-King,
> Author of glory,   created the world,

The earth and the heavens.   The music of its hymn .
Is sweeter than all song-craft,   more winsome and fair
Than any harmony.   Neither trumpet nor horn,
Nor melody of harp   is like to that lay,
Nor voice of man,   nor strain of organ music,
Nor swan's singing feathers,   nor any pleasant sound
That God gave for joy to men   in this mournful world.]

And even the usually terse Latin describes the uniqueness over a space of six lines:

> incipit illa sacri modulamina fundere cantus
>   et mira lucem voce ciere novam,
> quam nec aedoniae voces nec tibia possit
>   musica Cirrhaeis adsimulare modis,
> sed neque olor moriens imitari posse putetur
>   nec Cylleneae fila canora lyrae.
>
>   (45–50)

[. . . she begins to pour forth the notes of a holy chant and to summon the new day in a wondrous melody, which neither the voice of the nightingale nor the tuneful pipe with its Cirrhaean measures can match. But neither can the dying swan be deemed a rival, nor the melodious strings of the Cyllenean lyre.]

That in the English poem the song is intended to suggest the celestial music of the holy choir there can be no doubt. The allegorical part of the poem associates the sun with God, who shines amid heavenly multitudes, and song is associated with their praise of him. Even Lactantius, who may have written the poem before his conversion to Christianity, calls the song sacred, more beautiful than the pagan examples he cites. Yet something behind the religious intent seems to be at work. When the phoenix of the English poem soars in ecstatic song to meet the sun, it seems positively transformed by the meeting. It is the ecstatic moment of union with the sun, a fecund, conceiving moment that, I think, causes the phoenix to sing out in both poems. And this quasi-set piece, coming between the Menstrual and Birth Sequences in the poems, suggests a joyous song of conception.

Singing is generally, apart from the celebration of conception, an aspect of rites of menarche. For example, the Nootka ceremony, studied by Boas in British Columbia, had its "t'a'ma," singing and dancing performed by hired singers while the rest of the ritual is in progress;[1] the Basuto *pollo* includes singing and dancing[2] as does the Bemba *chisungu*;[3] and Zulu girls of South Africa sing puberty songs to initiates during their period of seclusion, accompanying the singing with clapping and

drum-beating.[4] But it should be pointed out that in the Swahili ceremony, as Velten notes particularly, dancing and singing *conclude* the
ritual celebrating menstruation. This places song in the Swahili rite just
where it falls in the poems: between menstruation and birth.[5] At the end
of their seclusion Swahili girls are carried on the shoulders of older
women and brought to the foot of the *muyombo* tree, the scene of a
festival of song and dance. The nubile girl is received by rejoicing young
women who honor her with a special dance known as the *kunguwia*.[6]
This rejoicing marks the girl's arrival at the threshold of the new stage to
which she has been brought by her passage through the menstrual
ritual; she is ready now to express her maturity by founding a family.
The singing that comes at the end of the menstrual ritual of Luvale
women is, as a consequence of its simplicity, even more dramatic.[7] Here
the emerging woman does the singing by herself. At the end of her
initiation she is seated on a stool in a shroud of mats from which she is
liberated by her parents who break the mats apart, calling out, "Uncover
our child!" Then the girl rises from her stool "singing 'Where am I to
look for my husband, mother?' "

Indeed, the ideal among many African tribes is for the woman to
marry her bethrothed immediately after her emergence from puberal
seclusion. The Tonga of Zambia, for instance, often terminated the girl's
menstrual ceremonies with her marriage to the man to whom she was
affianced.[8] Customarily the African woman who passes from nubile girl
to the status of wife is eager to promote fertility and childbirth. When
the Tonga woman is successful, her powers of fertility are recognized by
a new title: she is no longer a girl (*mooye*) but a woman (*mukaintu*).[9]
Among the Yakö of southeastern Nigeria, brides try to foster the
moment of conception by a strict regimen of good feeding and inaction
so protracted that one anthropologist has examined the behavior as a
"Marriage Ritual."[10]

Song, then, when placed at the end of menstrual rites, seems to herald
the sexual union that will follow initiation and produce offspring. The
possibility of conception is what sets the bride's friends "parading
through the town singing, dancing, and beating pans" when her husband, following Kanuri tradition, announces that the marriage is con-
summated.[11] Among the Chaga there is feasting, which includes singing
and dancing, when the union of husband and wife has actually led to
conception.[12]

A song that is taught to Bemba girls is of special interest, not because it
celebrates arrival at the threshold of womanhood after the menstrual
ceremonies are complete—it doesn't—but because of the song's subject:
the sun. According to Richards, it is a song of pregnancy that is learned
as part of the Bemba initiation training. The song's words are:

The sun has set;
The sun has already gone.
The days are fulfilled;
Let me go and honour the
musuku tree.[13]

The lyric appears to associate the sun with the growth of the child in the womb, or perhaps even to suggest that it is the cause of the child's growth in the womb; hence the concluding desire to go and venerate one of the women's trees, linked in Bemba lore to fertility. Like the phoenix perched aloft after its bath, the narrator of this lyric is preoccupied with watching the sun's movements. In the Old English poem, the sun, whose path is as closely marked, is the source of the bird's joy:

Ðonne bi∂ swā fæger   fugles gebæru,
onbryrded brēostsefa   blissum rēmig.

(125–26)

[Then is the bearing   of the bird so fair,
Its heart so gladsome   and so graced with joy].

The adverb *Ðonne*, which conveys the sense of "afterwards, thereafter," indicates that the meeting with the sun is what leads to the fair bearing, happy heart, and joyousness of the bird.

Sun (and Heat)

The image of the sun and all that it symbolizes scientifically and anthropologically within a generative context signals a clear demarcation between the Menstrual and Birth Sequences of the two poems. The sun is the central image of the Conception Sequence.

As we go on to consider the sun's role in generation and look now at what precedes the flood of song in the Latin poem, we are led to suspect that, at its core, the song owes as much to sexual as to religious ecstasy. The image of the sun's rays hitting the threshold of the glowing door just before the bird pours out its song,

atque ubi Sol pepulit fulgentis limina portae
  et primi emicuit luminis aura levis,
incipit illa sacri modulamina fundere cantus.

(43–45)

[And when the Sun has knocked at the threshold of the shining gate and the faint gleam of the first light has darted forth, she begins to pour forth the notes of a holy chant.]

not only strikes us as patently sexual but seems finally to have in its background a possible primitive relative in a Chaga song that forms part of the opening ceremonies of the tribe's female initiation rite. Raum reports this sung interchange between the novice's assistant and an older woman teacher seated in a shed where a fire is lit at the start of the ceremony. When the assistant arrives at the shed,

> she sings: *"Kichumi ngakuirikira, nyi mbeo ingirure!"* (i.e. Door, I greet you, I have been brought hither by the cold!) Then she sits down to receive an answer. After some time, one of the old women inside replies singing: "Who is at the door?," and after another interval: "Who was it who put the door there?" To this the novice's "elder sister" replies: "It is the chief! It is the Great God! It is he who made the door through which everyone has to pass!" The woman, pushing a firebrand into the ashes, sings: "Who is it who sticks the firebrand into the ashes?" The assistant replies: "It is the father, and the hearth is the mother. When the father places the firebrand in the hearth, the child emerges!"[14]

The image of the sun's rays striking the glowing door in Lactantius seems to echo the firebrand, door, and burning embers of this Chaga song and to evoke similar images that must have existed in earlier songs in which a primitive folk tried to explain the mystery of conception.

The bird's activities are closely tied to the sun. We see this when the bird watches for sunrise from the lofty tree (*Phoenix*, 111–19; *Carmen*, 40–44); flies up to meet the risen sun (*Phoenix*, 123); sings ecstatically while the sun shines (*Phoenix*, 127–42; *Carmen*, 45–50); and falls silent when it sets (*Phoenix*, 142–43; *Carmen*, 54). We will see the close ties between sun and phoenix also in the birth section of the poem where the bird is even called the sun's retainer (*þegn*, 288). Oliver T. Emerson rejected this reading in favor of *segn* because he felt the English poem excluded all connections with "Sun-idolatry."[15] Not only do I agree with Blake that "Emerson would hardly have made his claim if he had borne the allegory in mind," but I think he could not have failed to accept the reading, *þegn*, if he had considered how suited the generative dimension of the sun is to the theme of renewal.[16]

Primitive peoples and ancient thinkers speculated about the sun's effect on fertility and the growth of animal as well as vegetable life. Frazer cites many examples of girls being shut off from sun or firelight at puberty because of the belief that the sun can cause impregnation,[17] a belief that lies behind Hamlet's warning about Ophelia, "Let her not walk i' the sun. Conception is a blessing, but not as your daughter may conceive" (2.2.185–86). In his observations of the initiation of Ahta

(Nootka) Indian girls in British Columbia, Sproat notes that the initiates were kept from seeing sunlight or firelight, although the precaution was not very strictly enforced.[18] In Egypt, as is well known, Amenhotep IV introduced the worship of the sun as the one god, called Ra. Ra's role in generation is clearly expressed in these words from the hymn to the sun believed to have been composed by Amenhotep:

> Creator of the germ in woman,
> Maker of seed in man,
> Giving life to the son in the body of his mother,
> Soothing him that he may not weep,
> Nurse (even in the womb.)
> When the fledgling in the egg chirps in the shell
> Thou givest breath therein to preserve him alive,
> When thou has brought him together
> To the point of bursting out of the egg,
> He cometh forth from the egg
> To chirp with all his might . . . .[19]

While Ra created the "germ" and "seed" of ordinary Egyptian mortals, the god was said to be the husband of the Queen of Egypt. The pharaoh produced, therefore, by Ra's impregnation was styled Son of Ra.[20] An even more ancient Egyptian hymn contained in the "Chapter of the coming forth by day out of the netherworld" demonstrates how closely the phoenix was, in its early mythic manifestation as an aspect of Ra, the rising sun, associated with the sun's life-giving energies:

> I am the god Ra at his first appearing.
> I am the great god, who created himself,
> and created his name, lord of the gods, to
> whom not only of the gods is equal (?).
> I was yesterday, and I know the morrow;
> the place of combat of the gods was made when
> I spoke. I know the name of that great god
> who dwells within him.
> I am that great Phoenix who is in Heliopolis . . . .[21]

It is worth recalling, in light of this hymn, that when the phoenix soars in song during the conception section of the poem he is greeting the rising sun.

The opening song of the Chaga initiation ceremony, quoted earlier, wherein the older woman explains the mystery of the firebrand to the younger, clearly places this Bantu tribe in line with others that associate "sacred fire" with begetting children. Among the Bemba, also, fire is associated with generation and young girls are said to owe motherhood

Fragments of a Middle Predynastic Egyptian vase. It pictures departed souls as incarnate in dancers wearing bird head-masks. *(By permission of the Ashmolean Museum, Oxford.)*

to older women who make fire for them during the *chisungu* initiation. One of the most important songs of the maturation rite involves "begging for fire":

> Scratch! Scratch! [The operating of
> the fire sticks]
> How many children have you born[e]?[22]

While this song is sung, the young girls are told that they must take on the bearing of children from the older women who, rubbing fire sticks together, have the power of giving or witholding generative energy from them.

In Daryll Forde's examination of what he calls the Marriage Ritual of the Nigerian Yakö, the long process of gathering the marriage firewood clearly reflects an association made between fecundity and fire.[23] It is the bride's duty to collect the wood, and her chore is timed to coincide with the beginning of the main harvest. The notion of harvest fruitfulness is a continuous backdrop against which the gathering proceeds; the collecting, cutting, and piling of the marriage wood goes on for about a month as the harvest is gathered. To some extent the groom contributes to the bride's task, for he is charged with erecting the frame on which the wood is stacked. Fire-making is also associated with fertility by the paleoagriculturists of Australia. The unobtrusive marriage ritual of the Dieri of Australia, for example, is indicative.[24] They consider a man and his betrothed married after they have kindled a fire together with special fire sticks. These consist of the grooved "female" hearth stick and the "male" drill stick—complementary in fire-making.

Whereas primitive African beliefs regarding conception may have been a distinctive aspect of Lactantius's inheritance, ancient scientific theories of generation would have been part of a common repository of knowledge, accessible to Latin and Anglo-Saxon poet alike. The ancients have much to say about the influence of the sun and heat on generation. Ideas central to Aristotelian thinking on the generative nature of heat appear in his *On the Generation of Animals*, wherein he makes a careful distinction between fire and the heat of animals and of the sun. Aristotle poses the question, "Why does not the female accomplish generation all by itself and from itself?" and his answer is the pivot on which his views on the generation of animals turns—the female cannot provide "sentient Soul," that which distinguishes plant from animal and without which it is not possible for any part of the body to exist.[25] For Aristotle the essence of maleness is that "the male is the factor which produces the sentient Soul."[26] The reason, according to Aristotle, that the male has this power is *pneuma*, a "hot" substance contained in the semen that is the agent of fertility; *pneuma*, he says, is like the stars that, of course, include the sun:

> . . . the semen contains within itself that which causes it to be fertile—what is known as "hot" substance, which is not fire nor any similar substance, but the *pneuma* which is enclosed within the semen or foam-like stuff, and the natural substance which is in the *pneuma*; and this substance is analogous to the element which belongs to the stars. That is why fire does not generate any animal, and we find no animal taking shape either in fluid or solid substances while they are under the influence of fire; whereas the heat of the sun does effect generation, and so does the heat of animals which operates through the semen, but also any other natural residue which there may be has within it a principle of life. Considerations of this sort show us that the heat which is in animals is not fire and does not get its origin or principle from fire.[27]

The male principle, then, is seen as the cause of the sentient soul in animals and as chemically related to the sun. Earlier in this work, Aristotle expresses a more general parallel between maleness and the sun:

> By a "male" animal we mean one which generates in another, by "female" one which generates in itself. This is why in cosmology too they speak of the nature of the Earth as something female and call it "mother," while they give to the heaven and the sun and anything else of that kind the title of "generator" and "father."[28]

So evident is the productivity of women that the female had appeared to early peoples as sufficient in herself. Not until the physiological facts concerning generation became better understood in agricultural societies was the role of the begetter understood. Before then, as Lucretius, for example, observes, when men saw the eggs of birds hatching into chicks, or worms swarming out of the mud of Mother Earth, the female appeared to be the exclusive source of fecundity.[29] Like Aristotle, Lucretius criticizes the idea that sentient creatures can arise from insentient matter:

> Some will say that at any rate the sentient can come from the insentient by a transformation or by some sort of birth by which it is thrust out; it will be enough to demonstrate clearly to him that no birth takes place nor is anything changed unless there has previously been an act of union.[30]

What relationship sentience may bear to the sun or the heat of animals or the vital heat of the semen Lucretius does not say.

Lactantius is more specific. He is in agreement with Aristotle that every animal consists of soul, "the living principle," as well as body and that the material of the soul is contained in heat. As evidence he draws on the example of birds, familiar from Lucretius but used to demonstrate a different point:

> Though these [the offspring of birds] are full of thick moisture, unless they are cherished by creative [the artificer] heat, the moisture cannot become a body.[31]

Aristotle would say that what makes the heat creative is its connection to the element of the stars, fecund as the heat of fire is not. Though Lactantius does refer to this creative heat as "fire," he traces the origin of its generative powers to the heavens:

> . . . We, being a heavenly and immortal race, make use of fire, which is given to us as a proof of immortality, since fire is from heaven, and its nature, inasmuch as it is moveable and rises upward, contains the principle of life.[32]

More obviously derivative of Aristotelian thinking on the sun's influence on generation are the views of the thirteenth-century philosopher, St. Thomas Aquinas, who, in the *Summa*, acknowledges his indebtedness to Aristotle, to whom he continually refers as "the Philosopher." The passage below in which Aquinas discusses the work of generation is virtually a paraphrase of the passage, cited earlier, from *On Generation* wherein Aristotle explains the fecund properties of *pneuma*. Aquinas writes that generative energy

> is based on the (vital) spirit in the semen which is frothy, as is attested by its whiteness. In which spirit, moreover, there is a certain heat derived from the power of the heavenly bodies, by virtue of which the inferior bodies also act towards the production of the species. . . . And since in this (vital) spirit the power of the soul is concurrent with the power of a heavenly body, it has been said that *man and the sun generate man*.[33]

This last quoted phrase is also used by Aquinas in another place and there directly attributed to Aristotle's *Physics*. Discussing the sun's part in generation—"a place of moderate temperature is required for the production of man and other perfect animals"—Aquinas emphasizes the idea that the sun cannot act alone and, hence, function as a first cause: "Perfect animals, produced from seed, cannot be made by the sole power of a heavenly body, as Avicenna imagined, although the power of a heavenly body may assist by cooperation in the work of natural generation; for the Philosopher says [*Physics*, II, 2 (194^b 13)] "man and the sun beget man from matter."[34]

Many of the same thinkers who were fascinated by the myth of the phoenix's self-recreation were also fascinated by embryological matters. Ovid, Pliny, and Lactantius, for example, wrote about both, and the Book of Job[35] contains allusions to both.

For Lactantius the human being's need to propogate was the main divide between mortals and the gods:

> If the gods are immortal and eternal, what need is there of the other sex, when they themselves do not require succession, since they are always about to exist? For assuredly in the case of mankind and the other animals, there is no other reason for difference of sex and procreation and bringing forth except that all classes of living creatures, inasmuch as they are doomed to death by the condition of their mortality, may be preserved by mutual succession.[36]

Of the two most constant subjects that appear in ancient discussions of generation—menstruation and the sun (or heat)—Lactantius contributes most to the thinking on the role played by heat. A thought to which we will need to return when we consider the sun's igniting of the phoenix's "house" is Lactantius's view that, in order to animate life, heat must be accompanied by moisture:

> Heraclitus said that all things were produced from fire; Thales of Miletus from water. Each saw something [of the truth], and yet each was in error: for if one (element) only had existed, water could not have been produced from fire, nor, on the other hand, could fire from water, but it is more true that all things were produced from a mingling of the two. . . . Rightly, therefore, does Ovid [*Metamorph.* I, 430] say: "For when moisture and heat become mingled, they conceive and all things arise from these two." . . . on this account it was appointed by the ancients that marriage contracts should be ratified by the solemnity of fire and water.[37]

Hippocrates, too, while stressing the importance of heat in generation, indicates that moisture, together with heat, is needed to produce the bones and sinews of the fetus,

> moist and . . . kept in movement by the fire [of the soul]. Being in movement it gets inflamed and draws to itself its nourishment from the food and breath that enter the woman. At first, while it is still rare, this occurs equally throughout; but owing to the movement and the fire it dries and solidifies; as it solidifies it hardens all round, and the fire being imprisoned can no longer draw to itself its nourishment in sufficient quantity, while it does not expel the

breath owing to the hardness of its envelope. So it consumes the available moisture inside. Now the parts in the compacted dry mass that are solid in substance . . . as the moisture fails . . . become compact, and are called bones and sinews.[38]

Thus, when Shakespeare speaks in sonnet 19 of the "long liv'd Phoenix" as *burning* "in her blood," he is fixing on precisely the two elements necessary to generate its life: heat and moisture.[39] Is Shakespeare aware of these connotations? Very likely, since in general Shakespeare tends to emphasize the generation rather than the death of the phoenix. In *3 Henry VI*, for example, he speaks of the phoenix's ashes *bringing forth* (1. 4. 35), and in *The Two Noble Kinsmen* Shakespeare links the phoenix to the "innocent cradle" (1. 3. 70). At this point we approach considerations that, while developing from an attempt to explain the role played by the sun or heat in conception, go beyond that fecund moment to address the problem of the formation of the embryo. Although these views are not directly germane to the Conception Sequence, they form a necessary bridge to several embryonic images (i.e., the ball of ashes, the apple and worm) that predominate in the Birth Sequence, the focus of the next chapter. So that those images can be understood for what they are, the digression that follows is introduced first.

The key to understanding ancient thought on embryology is that early scientists regarded menstrual blood as the foundation of the embryo. The necessary moisture, acting in cooperation with the heat, which Lactantius and Hippocrates speak of in the passages above, would be identified by most ancient thinkers as menstrual blood. Indeed, in another work, *Generation*, Hippocrates identifies the "moisture" that flows into the fetus to coagulate and then form the embryonic flesh as the catamenia. Essentially this was the view of Aristotle, as well, who regarded the menstrual flow as the material from which the embryo's flesh was formed, for while the male provided the "form" and the "principle of movement,"[40] the female provided the "body" or "material":

> The contribution which the female makes to generation is the *matter* used therein, . . . this is to be found in the substance constituting the menstrual fluid. . . .[41]

Aristotle viewed semen as a kind of setting agent that acted by virtue of the *dynamis* supplied by its "vital heat":

> The action of the semen of the male in "setting" the female's secretion in the uterus is similar to that of rennet upon milk. Rennet is

milk which contains vital heat, as semen does, and this integrates
the homogeneous substance and makes it "set."[42]

Two passages of embryological importance in the Bible have been
cited as evidence that the Alexandrian Jews working on the wisdom
literature were influenced by Aristotle and, in one instance, by Hippocrates also.[43] In Job 10:9–11, Job echoes Aristotle's milk-curdling metaphor:

> You modeled me, remember, as clay is modeled,
>   and would you reduce me now to dust?
> Did you not pour me out like milk,
>   and curdle me then like cheese;
> Clothe me with skin and flesh,
>   and weave me of bone and sinew?[44]

The other embryological passage in the wisdom literature occurs in the
Wisdom of Solomon 7:2 and reflects the Aristotelian idea that the embryo is formed from the catamenia as well as the Hippocratic notion that
embryonic flesh is "compacted" blood:

> I was modeled in flesh within my mother's womb,
> for ten months taking shape in her blood
> by means of virile seed and pleasure, sleep's companion.

The significance herein is that by the third century B.C. Alexandrine Jews
were familiar with Aristotelian embryology. Thus, when the Alexandrine school introduced Greek medicine and biology to Rome, where
it eventually influenced men like Pliny and Lactantius, the corpus of
knowledge included Artistotle's views on generation. It is not surprising,
therefore, to hear Pliny sounding an Aristotelian note in the observation
that women without menstrual flow "do not have children, since the
substance in question is the material for human generation, as the semen
from the males acting like rennet collects this substance within, which
thereupon immediately is inspired with life and endowed with body."[45]

The Book of Sidrac(h),[46] an important source of medieval scientific lore,
as well as the pseudo-Aristotelian Secretum Secretorum[47] are surprisingly
silent on the Aristotelian concept that the seminal fluid for generation
was produced by the man, the female menses providing the passive
matter on which his seed acted. The view, however, became general in
the Roman world and was asserted by Augustine[48] as well as by later
writers, among them "the cursed monk" Constantine (b. 1087) whom
Geoffrey Chaucer refers to in The Canterbury Tales (CT, E:1809–11). Constantine writes of the semen that "it is a warm, runny spirit which
permeates the body's moisture and creates the generative power of the

man from whom it comes."[49] Also, this Aristotelian idea appears in the twenty or so scattered pages on procreation and birth that are found in Book 2 of *Causae et Curae* by the twelfth-century Saint Hildegard von Bingen, Benedictine Abbess of Rupertsberg. She writes that while the male provides the generative seed, the female's menstrual blood provides the warm, nourishing atmosphere in which the fetus can develop.[50] The same idea appears in an early fifteenth-century English scientific treatise containing material on obstetrics that seems to derive from Soranus of Ephesus, who practiced in Rome during the reigns of Trajan and Hadrian:[51]

> To women after þei be with
> child for to they be deliuered,
> thei ne haue nought þis
> purgacion for þe childe in her
> wombe is norisshed with þe
> blood þat þei shuld be purged
> of.[52]

From the Aristotelian viewpoint, then, the phoenix of the poems bathes in the very font and origin of life.

4

THE BIRTH SEQUENCE

The central aim of the discussion of what I call the Birth Sequence (*The Phoenix* 171–257; *Carmen*, 69–108) is to demonstrate by anthropological and other scientific evidence that not only the images in this portion of the poem but also the actions within the narrative structure—which elaborates, after all, a story of regeneration—are paralleled by rites, treatments, and ideas surrounding the mystery of birth in various cultures, especially in Africa, the country in which Lactantius was born. The images and the narrative motifs that will be explored in this section of the study include: sun, fumigation, ball of ashes, apple and worm, seed, seclusion, escort and ring, and, finally, manifestation of the bird.

Sun

As the Birth Sequence opens, the sun image reappears. Aloft in a palm tree—a phoenix palm—the bird enjoys conditions that were believed by the ancients and scientists of the Middle Ages to be favorable to successful pregnancy. The description of the full light of the sun shining down upon the phoenix in its nest occupies about one-tenth of the Old English sequence and about one-eighth of the Latin. Eight lines of the Birth Sequence of *The Phoenix* include sun imagery:

> hlūttor heofones gim   hālig scīneð,
>
> (183)

> [. . . heaven's bright gem   shines holy on high.]

>   . . . sūþan blīceð
> wedercondel wearm,   weorodum lȳhteð,
>
> (186–87)

> [. . . the weather-candle   shines warm from
>   the south.]

> Siteð sīþes fūs.   Þonne swegles gim,
> on sumeres tīd   sunne hātost
> ofer sceadu scīneð   ond gesceapu drēogeð,

woruld geondwlīteð,   þonne weorðeð his
hūs onhǣted   þurh hādor swegl.

(208–12)

[When the gem of the sky   in the summer season,
The burning sun,   shines over the shades
Scanning the world,   the Phoenix sits
Fair of departure,   fulfilling his fate.
His house is kindled   by heat of the sun.]

And a space of five lines in the forty-line Latin *Carmen* sequence is taken up with sun description. Aeolus is said to confine the winds lest

neu concreta Noto nubes per inania caeli
   submoveat radios solis et obsit avi.

(75–76)

[a cloud, gathered by the South Wind through the voids of heaven, may shut off the sun's rays and stay the bird.]

interea corpus genitali morte peremptum
   aestuat, et flammam parturit ipse calor,
aetherioque procul de lumine concipit ignem:
   flagrat, et ambustum solvitur in cinerem.

(95–98)

[Meantime her body, destroyed by a lifegiving death, grows warm; and the very heat produces a flame. From the far-off heavenly light it takes fire. It blazes and, consumed, is reduced to ashes.]

The full light of the sun provides the heat—ultimately turning into creative fire—that primitive peoples as well as early scientists recognized as playing an essential role in generation (cp. "Sun (and Heat)," chapter 3).

Blake, pointing to the Anglo-Saxon poet's "tendency to anthropomorphize the phoenix in the first half,"[1] cites specifically the description used for the bird's nest: "In the first half it is most commonly referred to as a *hus*, otherwise as a *solere*, a *willsele*, a *hof* and twice as a *nest*. In this house the bird *gewicað* 'encamps' as any human being might."[2] The effect of the reference to human houses and halls, Blake concludes, is to strengthen "the allegorical correspondences between the birds and the human habitat."[3] While this effect is clear to see, and has, for instance, won the approval of Cross, who refers to Blake's observation in his own classic article on *The Phoenix*, it is not the only effect produced by the anthropomorphic technique of the poet. As Cross himself asserts about Blake's assumption that the poet rewrote the story in the light of the allegory, "The facts he presents do warrant such a conclusion but, to my mind, do not explain other difficulties: why, for example, . . . the retinue of birds on the way to Syria is inserted and not explained, and so on."[4] Some of these problems may, perhaps, be solved by the realization that a second effect is also produced by the anthropomorphizing tendency of the Anglo-Saxon poet: it reinforces a comparison between the process of generating the bird and that of generating human beings. Ultimately the "whole story of the flight of the phoenix to Syria and its death there in a palm tree"[5] is Lactantius's invention, but the Anglo-Saxon poet unquestionably has gone a long way toward humanizing it.

Fumigation

One of the first effects of the sun's heat is the production of fragrant steam amidst the herbs the phoenix has collected and placed around itself as a nest. I consider this steam the second element of the Birth Sequence and, from the perspective of the birth process about to begin, it might best be called a "fumigation" system. The imagery of steam, redolent with scent, suggests steamy fumigation, an external expedient that has been used to facilitate delivery by many peoples in many times. The Ebers papyrus, the earliest document of Egyptian gynecology, written during the reign of Amenhotep (1550 B.C.), recommends the use of fennel, incense, garlic, sert-juice, and fresh salt to induce labor.[6] In the Hippocratic method of fumigation, used throughout the Middle Ages, vapors produced by boiling herbs and liquid were introduced directly into the womb.[7] Pliny's *Natural History*, a work read steadily throughout the Middle Ages, recommends garlic for fumigating the womb together with "whole eggs, with rue, dill and cumin taken in wine"[8] to make childbirth easier. In medieval Germany fumigations of the women in labor were accomplished in the following manner: "Over a brazier a funnel was placed, or the apparatus was so constructed that the funnel was part of the coal pan. This apparatus was placed under a chair in which the woman sat."[9]

The aromatic herbs described by Lactantius are numerous and exotic:

> colligit hinc sucos et odores divite silva,
>   quos legit Assyrius, quos opulentus Arabs,
> quos aut Pygmaeae gentes aut India carpit
>   aut molli generat terra Sabaea sinu.
> cinnamon hic auramque procul spirantis amomi
>   congerit et mixto balsama cum folio:
> non casiae mites nec olentis vimen acanthi

nec turis lacrimae guttaque pinguis abest.
his addit teneras nardi pubentis aristas
    et sociat myrrae vim, panacea, tuam.

(*Carmen*, 79–88)

[Here she collects juices and perfumes from the fruitful
wood, such products as the Assyrian gathers or the rich
Arab, as either the Pygmy nations or India harvests, or
Sheba's land produces in its soft bosom. Here the Phoenix
piles cinnamon, the fragrance of far-smelling amomum,
and balsam, together with a mixture of nard. Nor is gentle
cassia and the twig of the odorous acanthus missing, or
tears of incense and its rich drop. To these she adds tender
shoots of full-grown nard and combines with myrrh thy
pungency, panacea.]

The reference to sweet balm and drops of oil in this passage suggests
that some of the aromatics might even be unguents, also commonly used
to aid delivery. A corresponding description of the gathering of herbs in
the Old English poem is briefer and more general:

            Þonne feor ond nēah
þā swētestan   somnað ond gædrað
wyrta wynsume   ond wudublēda
tō þām eardstede,   æþelstenca gehwone,
wyrta wynsumra   þe Wuldorcyning,
Fæder frymða gehwæs   ofer foldan gescōp
tō indryhtum   ælda cynne
swētes under swegle. . . .

                                                    (192–99)

            [. . . From near and far
He gleans and gathers   to his lodging-place
Pleasant plants   and fruits of the forest,
All sweetest spices   and fragrant herbs
Which the King of glory,   Lord of beginnings,
Created on earth   for a blessing to men,
The sweetest under heaven. . . .]

However, the poet goes on to indicate more explicitly the steamy use the
herbs are put to in fumigations:

Wyrta wearmiað,   willsele stýmeð
swētum swæccum, ...

                                                    (213–14)

[The herbs grow hot,   the pleasant hall steams
With sweetest odours, ...]

"willsele," suggesting far more a room in which to give birth than a nest.[10]

Practices used well into the early twentieth century in places as remote from one another as East Prussia and the White Nile are quite similar to the medieval procedure. The Prussians commonly seated the woman in labor over a vessel of hot camomile tea, while the Kerrie Negroes made the woman near delivery stand above a hole in which a fire had been kindled below a concoction of herbs.[11] Similarly, Australian aboriginal women assisted their fellow tribeswomen in labor by steaming them over a kind of stove, the *bangi*.[12] Besides herbal fomentations, the anointing of the female genitals before delivery has long been an obstetric procedure. Hippocrates recommended the oiling of the vagina (*De morbis mulierum* 1.15),[13] and his advise was followed over a long period of time by diverse peoples—by, for example, Avicenna, German doctors of the Middle Ages, and early midwives. In an early fifteenth-century English gynecological handbook, "thyme oil, pure lily oil, or oil of musk,"[14] rubbed on the hand of the midwife, are suggested as useful aids to the delivery of babies that present themselves in unusual positions. Later, in a handbook written for early seventeenth-century midwives, we find the following instructions:

> Last of all the midwife shall set down before the woman and smear the foremost parts of the womb with oil of white lilies, sweet almond oil and poultry fat mixed together.[15]

The distance between the "oil of white lilies" and "sweet almond oil" here referred to and Lactantius's sweet balm and drops of oil is slight.

Ball of Ashes

The third element of the Birth Sequence, the ball of ashes, is the first embryonic image of the poems. Just before the phoenix is reborn, the old phoenix is burned to ashes. In the Old English poem we are told that the bird's house, which is to say its body, is kindled by the sunlight: ". . . þonne weorðeð his / hūs onhæted   þurh hādor swegl" (211–12, "His house is kindled by heat of the sun"). Lactantius's description of the sun's creation of fire conveys, through the suggestiveness of the word "concipit," a *fecund* fire: "Aetherioque procul de lumine concipit ignem" (97, "From the far-off heavenly light it takes fire"). In another place, it will be recalled, Lactantius wrote more directly about the generative potential of fire:

> Fire . . . inasmuch as it is moveable and rises upward, contains the principle of life.[16]

In both poems the effect of fire is not merely to turn the bones and flesh of the old phoenix to ashes but simultaneously to revitalize them as they become compacted into a ball. It seems clear to me that the notion of the aggregation of the ashes found in both the Old English poem (". . . yslan . . . lūcan tōgædre / geclungne tō clēowenne. . . ." [224–26, "Ashes . . . fusing together / Compressed to a ball]) and Lactantius ("quos velut in massam, generans in morte, coactos / conflat, et effectum seminis instar habet" [99–100, "Engendering in death, she gathers and moulds these ashes into a mass, as it were, and as a result produces something like a seed"]) must derive from Hippocrates's idea that the flesh of the embryo forms from the coagulation of menstrual blood and its becoming compacted into a dry mass.[17] Apart from the emphasis on aggregation in the poems, there are two other reasons for viewing the compacted ashes as embryonic: (1) in the case of Lactantius, "in morte" (99) has been read by some scholars[18] as "umore" ("moisture"), which alters the reading to "Quos velut in massam, generans umore coactos" and thus suggests the coagulation of menstrual blood even more strongly; and (2) the Anglo-Saxon poet would know that in Ambrose's *Hexameron*[19] (bk. 5, ch. 79–80), a source for lines 443ff.,[20] the phoenix is said to die after entering a "theca" of frankincense and myrrh. One of the Latin synonyms for *theca* is *vagina*. One commentator on the phoenix legend who begins to address the problem of the aggregated ashes in Lactantius, Van den Broek, concludes that "the ashes [are] serving the phoenix as semen."[21] Although it is tempting to identify "seminis" (100) as semen, it is more logical to get to the creature without limbs (101) from a mass that is like the germ of an embryo (100) than from diffuse semen. Although the phoenix reproduces asexually, lines 230–36 of *The Phoenix*,

> Þonne of þām āde   æples gelīcnes
> on þāre ascan bið   eft gemēted,
> of þām weaxeð wyrm,   wundrum fæger,
> swylce hē of ǣgerum,   ūt ālǣde
> scīr of scylle.   Þonne on sceade weaxeð
> þæt hē ǣrest bið   swylce earnes brid,
> fæger fugeltimber; . . . .

> [From the flame of the fire   is found thereafter
> In the ash of the pyre   an apple's likeness,
> Of which grows a worm,   more wondrous fair,
> As it were a creature   come from an egg,
> Shining from the shell . . . .]

and lines 99–108 of the *Carmen*,

> quos velut in massam, generans in morte, coactos
> conflat, et effectum seminis instar habet.

hinc animal primum sine membris fertur oriri,
    sed fertur vermi lacteus esse color.
crescit, et emenso sopitur tempore certo,
    seque ovi teretis colligit in speciem.
ac velut agrestes, cum filo ad saxa tenentur,
    mutari tineae papilione solent,
inde reformatur qualis fuit ante figura,
    et Phoenix ruptis pullulat exuviis.

[Engendering in death, she gathers and molds these ashes into a mass, as it were, and as a result produces something like a seed. Men say that from it a living thing without limbs first arises; but the worm, they say, is milky-white in color. It grows, and after it has passed a fixed time, it slumbers and takes on the semblance of a rounded egg.

And just as chrysalids in the country, when holding themselves to stones with a thread, are wont to change into a butterfly, from this worm is formed anew a body such as the bird had before. The Phoenix, bursting her shell, comes forth.]

clearly describe the early embryological development of a chick—known since the Hippocratic school to resemble that of mammals.[22]

Evidently, not all the ashes of the old phoenix are used to form the embryo of the new bird, for some remains of the old phoenix's bones and flesh are reclaimed by the young phoenix. In the Old English poem the reborn bird takes the ashy remains of the old bird and buries them in its garden home (*The Phoenix*, 267–87), while in the Latin poem the renewed phoenix brings a ball of remains to an altar in the City of the Sun (*Carmen*, 117–22). Both of these treatments may derive from various rituals connected with the disposal of the afterbirth. Among many African tribes, it is buried in the floor of the birth hut or close by in a special area of the tribe's compound.[23] Nearly as often, however, these exuviae are not buried but are placed in the custody of a trusted individual, usually a relative.[24] It may be that the priests of the temple in the City of the Sun perform a function that parallels that of the guardian relative.

Apple and Worm

The fourth element of the Birth Sequence brings us to what are actually two images—the apple and the worm—but since they are so closely related, I will treat them as one element.

In an interesting examination of several images in the Old English poem, Joanne Kantrowitz identifies the apple as just that—an apple—on

which a silkworm generates spontaneously as "such worms are generated in vegetable matter."[25] Somehow this silkworm metamorphoses
into a winged insect and then into a true bird. Although the silkworm is
seductive since it is a symbol of the resurrection of the soul and so would
fit thematically, the progression traced by Kantrowitz from the silkworm
is less straightforward than that in the poem, which, as we shall see,
depends on a fundamental understanding of fetal development.

Equally as roundabout an interpretation of the worm as a silkworm is
the view that the worm signifies that the Old English poem proposes
spontaneous generation from the dead phoenix. Although worms referred to in early versions of the phoenix legend (i.e., St. Clement the
Roman's *First Epistle to the Corinthians*,[26] Ambrose's *Hexameron*) have
certainly set scholars theorizing about generation from putrefaction
fluid,[27] it should be borne in mind that when the ancients saw maggots
form, as they thought, "spontaneously" in the dead flesh of a horse, the
maggots turned into flies, not horses. But the worm in the phoenix's
compressed, applelike ashes does become a phoenix, not some other
thing. As Aquinas observed, the distinct thing about spontaneous generation is that there is dissimilarity between generator and generated:

> A worm which is generated from animals has not the aspect of
> generation and sonship, although it has a generic likeness; for the
> notion of this kind of generation requires that there should be a
> procession by way of likeness in the same specific nature, as a man
> proceeds from a man.[28]

To understand why "sonship" *is* involved in the phoenix's development
from the worm, we must reconsider the apple image.

Since the general shape of the apple is round and since it is found in
the ashes of the pyre (*The Phoenix*, 230–31) it is probably identifiable as
that same compressed ball (227) that I have already suggested should be
considered an embryo. There are ancient precedents for associating the
embryo with fruit. Plutarch of Chaeronea, for example, reports of Stoic
thinking on the development of the embryo:

> The Stoicks say that it is a part of the wombe and not an animall by
> itselfe. For like as fruits be parts of trees, which when they be ripe
> do fall, even so it is with an infant in the mother's wombe.[29]

Likewise in the writings of the Talmud, produced between the second
and sixth centuries A.D., the embryo was referred to as a fruit: *peri
habbetten*, "fruit of the body."[30] (We will need to return to this idea of fruit
when we come to an allegorical consideration of the apple image in
chapter 5.) It is interesting to observe further of Talmudic embryology

that the first embryonic stage was called *golem*, "formless, rolled-up thing." The "rolled-up" aspect of the *golem* suggests, on the one hand, the layered nature of the ashes compressed into a ball in the Old English poem (227) while, on the other hand, the feature of "formlessness" brings to mind Lactantius's ashes coming together in a mass (99).

By the time the worm grows from the apple in the Old English poem an advanced stage of embryonic development is clearly attained, since the worm is likened to a creature that has emerged from its shell (230–34). Although the word "wyrm" is a problem in that it is usually associated with the reptilian in Old English, the egg-hatching simile here helps bring to mind a featherless chick, so young as still to bear that distinctively embryonic "curved-back" look. The creature, by the time it is described with the word "fugeltimber" (236), must be a sizable bird, more developed than is suggested by A. S. Cook's note—"the half-formed condition of the incipient bird"—as the bird in its fully formed state is like an eagle:[31]

> . . . ðonne furþor gin
> wrīdað on wynnum   þæt hē bið wæstmum gelīc
> ealdum earne, . . .
>
> (236–38)

> [. . . then flourishing fair
> Is like in form   to a full-grown eagle.]

The milk-white worm described by Lactantius is also the embryonic bird, curved within its shell until it has grown large enough to emerge: "Et Phoenix ruptis pullulat exuviis" (106; "And from the broken shell the Phoenix springs"). Usually the milk-white worm is identified by scholars as the larva of a butterfly, but that is to confuse the object with the thing to which it is compared.[32] A comparison to a butterfly does not suggest it is a butterfly; Lactantius merely develops an analogy between the growth of the phoenix and the progress of the larva to the stages of caterpillar and butterfly:

> hinc animal primum sine membris fertur oriri,
>   sed fertur vermi lacteus esse color.
> crescit, et emenso sopitur tempore certo,
>   seque ovi teretis colligit in speciem.
> ac velut agrestes, cum filo ad saxa tenentur,
>   mutari tineae papilione solent
> inde reformatur qualis fuit ante figura,
>   et Phoenix ruptis pullulat exuviis.
>
> (101–8)

[Men say that from it a living thing without limbs first arises; but the worm, they say, is milky-white in color. It grows, and after it has passed a fixed time, it slumbers and takes on the semblance of a rounded egg.

And, just as chrysalids in the country, when holding themselves to stones with a thread, are wont to change into a butterfly, from this worm is formed anew a body such as the bird had before. The Phoenix, bursting her shell, comes forth.]

The parallelism works allegorically as well as zoologically since the butterfly, like the phoenix, is a traditional symbol of resurrection and since the development of the egg was recognized by ancient science to resemble that of larvae: for example, Aristotle observes, "The growth of the egg is like [that of] larvae, for those animals which produce larvae produce something small to start with, which grows by its own means and not in virtue of any attachment."[33] Lactantius's description of the phoenix's rebirth ends here; the Anglo-Saxon poet, however, adds an extended seed simile:

>   Þonne brǣd weorþeð
> eal ednīwe   eft ācenned,
> synnum āsundrad.   Sumes onlīce
> swā mon tō ondleofne   eorðan wæsmas
> on hærfeste,   hām gelǣdeð
> wiste wynsume   ǣr wintres cyme
> on rypes tīman,   þȳ læs hī rēnes scūr
> āwyrde under wolcnum;   þær hī wraðe mētað,
> fōdorþege gefēon   þonne forst ond snāw
> mid ofermaegne   eorþan þeccað
> wintergewǣdum;   of þām wæstmum sceal
> eorla ēadwelan   eft ālǣdan
> þurh cornes gecynd,   þe ǣr clǣne bið
> sǣd onsāwen,   þonne sunnan glǣm,
> on lenctenne   līfes tācen
> weceð woruldgestrēon   þæt þā wæstmas bēoð,
> þurh āgne gecynd   eft ācende
> foldan frætwe;   swā se fugel weorþeð
> gomel æfter gēarum   geong ednīwe
> flǣsce bifongen . . . .

                                    (240–59)

>   [. . . Then is beauty reborn,
> Sundered from sin,   once more made new;
> Even in such fashion   as men, for food,
> Bring home in harvest   at reaping time

Pleasant fare,   the fruits of earth,
Ere coming of winter   lest rain-storms waste;
Find joy and strength   in their garnered store
When frost and snow   with furious might
Cover earth over   with winter weeds;
From these grains again   grow riches for men
Through the sprouting kernels,   first sowed pure seed.
Then the warm sun in Spring Time,   symbol of life,
Wakes the world's wealth   And new crops rise,
Each after its kind,   the treasures of earth.
Even so the Phoenix   after long life
Grows young and fashioned   with flesh anew.]

Seed

Like Lactantius's butterfly, the fifth element of the Birth Sequence—
the seed simile—has dual appropriateness. First, the seed image, originating in 1 Corinthians 15:36–38,

> Whatever you sow in the ground has to die before it is given new life
> and the thing that you sow is not what is going to come; you sow a
> bare grain, say of wheat or something like that, and then God gives
> it the sort of body that he has chosen: each sort of seed gets its own
> sort of body.

was widely used by the Fathers of the Church as a resurrection metaphor. Secondly, the passage draws on a long tradition depicting woman
as a field in which seed was sown, a tradition that manifests itself in
literature as well as in ritual behavior. E. S. Hartland[34] and S. A. Cook[35]
list examples of the farmland metaphor in Vedic, Egyptian, and Hebrew
sources. It would be easy to add many examples to their lists, but
nothing would be gained by extensive illustration that could not be
indicated by several representative instances of the metaphor. Galen
likens the womb receiving seed to earth in *On the Natural Faculties:*

> The seed having been cast into the womb or into the earth (for there
> is no difference) then, after a certain definite period, a great number
> of parts become constituted in the substance which is being gener-
> ated.[36]

Similar metaphors are used in *De Rerum Natura*, wherein Lucretius
speaks of "Venus sowing the field of woman," "atque in eost Venus ut
muliebria conseratarva" (4.1107),[37] and in *Antigone*, where the following
interchange appears,

Ismene.   Then you will kill the wife your son has chosen?

Creon.   Yes. There are other fields that he can plough.[38] (522–23)

Similarly, in *Seven Against Thebes* Aeschylus says that Oedipus "dared to sow seed in the sacred furrow where he was himself formed, and plant there a bloody branch"[39] (750ff.). Shakespeare uses the same image in *Antony and Cleopatra*, where it is said of Cleopatra

> Royal Wench!
> She made great Caesar lay his sword to bed.
> He plowed her, and she cropped.[40]
>
> (2.2. 231–33)

Not only may a part of the woman be used for comparison to the receptive earth, but, as we can see in the Anglo-Saxon passage below, the earth may be likened to the whole woman. In this example the woman is the Earth Mother whose body receives the embrace of the gods:

> Hal wesþu, folde, fira modor,
> beo þu ʒrowende on ʒodes fæþme,
> fodor gefylled firum to nytte.
>
> [Hail, Earth, Mother of men,
> be fertile in the gods' embrace,
> be filled with fruit for man's use.][41]

This spell could, perhaps, be discussed as ritual behavior reflecting a perceived relationship between human and agricultural fertility, for the spell, and others like it, must actually have been used by the Anglo-Saxons in times of scarcity when the land was barren. The spell is not unlike certain garden mimes performed by the Bemba during their female initiation ceremonies. However, because of the occasion of the mimes, it is hard to know if they are intended, like the Anglo-Saxon spell, to make the gardens grow or to "teach the girls to garden" in a metaphoric sense. In one of the garden mimes female initiates are made to take turns hoeing the ground while older women mime the gesture with their arms in time with a song that urges young girls to cultivate their gardens.[42] Throughout, the parallel references of hoe and husband, garden and girl are implicit. The Yakö practice of gathering marriage firewood, cited earlier, might usefully be recalled now for the light it sheds on the tradition in ritual behavior of relating the productivity of women with the productivity of the land.[43] This marriage ritual, intended to insure a fruitful union, is always timed to occur simultaneously with the gathering of the crops at harvest season. Characteristically, these activities proceed in tandem for about a month.

Possibly related to the earth-woman parallel in initiation ritual is the scarification pattern given girls at puberty by the Tiv of Nigeria, a West African Bantu tribe. Although the Tiv themselves regard the scars as purely decorative, Bruce Lincoln in *Emerging from the Chrysalis* discusses them as a female initiation ritual, for the effect of the scarification "is transformative: it is the means whereby a girl becomes a woman, and the mark of this transformation is the girl's laughter at her former companions who have not yet been scarified."[44] Significantly, the scars are said to promote fertility, not merely that of human life, but that of agricultural life as well, and among the Tiv it is the woman who is responsible for tending crops. Lincoln observes that "responsibility for the fertility of the people and crops . . . devolves upon Tiv women when they receive the scars."[45] A linguistic connection between the scarified woman and agricultural fertility is made by the Tiv word for a typical vertical line in the scarification design: *nongo*. The word applies equally to a line running from the throat to the navel and to a ridge on which crops are to be grown.[46]

Considered within the context of this woman-earth parallel, the extended seed simile in *The Phoenix* invites us, if we are cognizant of the relationship early peoples perceived between menstruation and the land, to examine the text for possible thematic and structural overlapping between the Menstrual and Birth Sequences of the poem. Although it is well known that primitive peoples and ancient thinkers believed menstruous women had a baleful influence on growing things, there is also evidence for the very opposite belief. In an early issue of the *Proceedings of the Royal Society of Medicine*, Raymond Crawfurd[47] calls attention to the following passage from Pliny:

> If a woman strips herself naked while she is menstruating and walks round a field of wheat, the caterpillars, wolves, beetles, and other vermin will fall off from the ears of corn. Metrodorus of Scepsos tells us that the discovery was first made in Cappadocia, and that, in consequence of such multitudes of cantharides being found to breed there, it is the practice for women to walk through the middle of the fields with their garments tucked up above the thighs. In other places, again, it is the usage for women to go barefoot, with the hair dishevelled and the girdle loose; due precaution must be taken, however, that this is not done at sunrise, for if so, the crop would wither up and dry up. (*Natural History* 28.23)

Evidently, the intimate relationship between the female and Nature here described is one in which the selectively negative effect of the menstrual flow causes insect life to suffer and vegetation to thrive.

As we come to the last four elements of the Birth Sequence in the Old English poem, we see that they do, indeed, seem to reflect *menstrual* ritual behavior: seclusion, the escort, the ring image, and the manifestation—and these elements, excepting the escort, are shared by the Latin poem.

Seclusion

The early sections of both phoenix poems emphasize the solitary nature of the bird's life in the remote woodland garden where daily the bird bathes and watches alone the sun's movement through the sky from its perch on a lofty tree. This emphasis on seclusion is repeated in both poems when the bird seeks a secret place in Syria where it will be reborn. Characteristically cogent, Lactantius observes that the phoenix seeks out a remote, secret place in the dense part of the forest where it can find a lofty palm tree:

> dirigit in Syriam celeres longaeva volatus,
> Phoenices nomen cui dedit ipsa vetus,
> secretosque petit deserta per avia lucos,
> sicubi per saltus silva remota latet.
> tum legit aerio sublimem vertice palmam,
> quae Graium phoenix ex ave nomen habet
>
> (65–70)

> [The aged bird directs her swift flight to Syria, upon which the original Phoenix bestowed the name Phoenicia. Along trackless wastes she seeks secluded groves, wheresoever through the glens a far-off wood lies hidden. Next she chooses a palm with top towering high in air, a tree which derives its Greek name "phoenix" from the bird.]

The Anglo-Saxon poet enlarges the idea of seclusion and also lengthens the journey. Few commentators bother to observe that in the Old English poem the phoenix makes his trip to Syria in two stages.[48] First the phoenix goes to a wasteland where no one lives and is there served by many other birds:

> Ðonne bið gehefgad   haswigfeðra
> gomol gēarum frōd.   Grēne eorðan,
> āflȳhð fugla wyn   foldan geblōwene

ond þonne gesēceð   sīde rīce
middangeardes,   þær nō men būgað,
eard ond ēþel.   Þær hē ealdordōm
onfēhð foremihtig   ofer fugla cynn
geþungen on þēode,   ond þrāge mid him
wēsten weardað. . . .

(153–61)

[. . . Aged and old
The gray-plumed is weary   and weighted with years.
Then the fairest of fowls   flies from the greenwood,
The blossoming earth,   seeks a boundless realm,
A land and lodging   where no man dwells;
And there exalted   over all the host
Has dominion and rule   of the race of birds,
With them in the waste   resides for a season.]

The concourse of birds accompanies the phoenix to Syria, but is driven off in the phoenix's move toward still greater isolation:

     . . . Him se clǣna þær
oðscūfeð scearplīce   þæt hē in scade weardað
on wudubearwe   wēste stōwe
biholene ond bihȳdde   hæleþa monegum.
Ðær hē hēanne bēam   on holtwuda
wunað ond weardað   wyrtum fæstne
under heofumhrōfe, . . .

(167–73)

[. . . There the pure fowl
Suddenly leaves them,   lodging in shadow
In a woodland covert,   a secret spot,
Sequestered and hidden   from the hosts of men.
There he takes lodging   in a lofty tree
Fast by its roots   in the forest-wood
Under heaven's roof. . . .]

Why do both poems strike the note of seclusion a second time? And, to take up one of Cross's questions, "why the retinue of birds on the way to Syria . . ."?[49] It seems to me that some of the answers may reside in the anthropological context. And, as we shall see in the following chapters, some additional light may also be shed on these problems when we reconsider the allegory from a different angle.

Among primitive peoples seclusion accompanies not only menstruation but childbirth as well. For example, in an early account of the customs of the Kisami tribe in Angola, an anthropologist writes:

When her confinement is near, the woman, as is the custom among many primitive tribes, leaves the house, since she has the idea that neither man nor woman should see her. She goes without anyone's knowing into the wood, where she stays by herself till she is delivered. Shortly after delivery she returns to the hut.[50]

Birth out-of-doors and alone is the tradition also among the Wakumbu and Wanyamwezi tribes of Central Africa, where women retire into the jungle to deliver their babies.[51] In South Africa most native villages contain special birth huts where women close to delivery are confined and where no man is permitted to enter.[52] These birth huts have a European analogue in ancient Greece: Pausanias speaks of certain birth establishments, the first of which were constructed in Epidaurus near the shrine of Asclepius, where women in labor were secluded.[53] Each of these selected examples testifies to the fact that early peoples regarded women in labor—like menstruating women—to be undergoing a mysterious process that set them apart from men and to which the proper response was a mixture of awe, fear, and, perhaps, even abhorrence. While each example provides a parallel to the recurring seclusion motif in the birth sections of both phoenix poems, none of them helps us with the problem of the escort in the Old English poem.

Escort and Ring

What are we to make of the escort? My earlier discussion of primitive ceremonies surrounding menarche indicated that old women of various African tribes—i.e., the Bemba, Chaga, Swahili, and Basuto—served as instructresses to the young female initiates and guided the ritual through its traditional stages. The reflection of such an escort would be out of place in the Birth Sequence of the Old English poem but it might be tempting to explain lines 167–73 and especially the *"preludium,"* lines 153–61, as an oral formulaic theme that is being repeated. Menstrual and Birth Sequences contain several features in common: a remote woodland, a lofty tree, and a solitary phoenix. To these we might even add songs of praise, since the description of general rejoicing and singing that greets the reborn bird on its return (*The Phoenix*, 335 ff; *Carmen*, 151 ff.) parallels the phoenix's earlier caroling to the risen sun (*The Phoenix*, 127–39; *Carmen*, 45–50) after the end of the Menstrual Sequence. That the *"preludium"* to the birth section includes, in the bird escort, a feature proper to the menstrual section and not to that about birth, however, cannot be regarded as the kind of misplaced overlap commonly found in oral compositions. First of all, the Anglo-Saxon poet follows the Latin poem too closely for him to have invented just this one detail while he appears to be repeating all the other presumably "misplaced overlappings" directly from the Latin poem. Indeed, besides the wood, tree, and solitary motifs, there are other features that turn up in the Birth Sequence of the two poems that might seem more appropriate to the Menstrual Sequence. There is, for instance, the circle of feathers around the phoenix's neck:

> Is ymb þone swēoran,   swylce sunnan hring,
> bēaga beorhtast   brogden feðrum.
>
> (305–6)

> [All round the neck   like the ring of the sun
> Is a shining circlet   fashioned of feathers.]

The figure of the circle, echoed in the comparison to the ring of the sun, has its genesis, I think, in the ceremonies of initiation in which necklaces and bracelets often appear. For example, at the end of the Bemba rite of transition described by Richards, bracelets of grass are put around the girls' arms.[54] In the Basuto *pollo* ceremony, recounted by K. Endemann, female initiates are made to dive into a stream and fish out bracelets.[55] Circular jewelry is an aspect not only of African but of Indian rituals as well. A. W. Painter, a nineteenth-century anthropologist, reports of the Arrians, inhabitants of the of the hills of Travancore, that the young girl's paternal aunt places a decorative string or thread around her niece's neck at the end of the initiation.[56] It is significant, in the light of this jewelry ritual, that in the Old English passage in which the circle image appears the phoenix is described in terms of an object crafted by artisans. A parallel image in Lactantius's poem seems to be that of the radiant crown:

> aptata est noto capiti radiata corona,
> Phoebi referens verticis alta decus.
>
> (139–40)

> [. . . a radiant crown
> Surrounds its head, like the bright rays that make
> The glorious insignia of the sun.]

The context here again suggests the jeweler or artist. Several lines before the reference the Latin poet speaks of shining gold, ivory, gems, and twin sapphires, and, several lines after, we are told a replica of the marvelous bird is sculpted in marble. And there is, as well, the matter of the manifestation of the bird, a feature that deserves separate attention.

Manifestation

In the poem by Lactantius, the forms of worshipping the reborn phoenix include not merely sculpting the bird in marble but also singing songs of praise and offering gifts:

> contrahit in coetum sese genus omne volantum,
> nec praedae memor est ulla nec ulla metus.
> alituum stipata choro volat illa per altum,
> turbaque prosequitur munere laeta pio.
>
> (*Carmen*, 155–58)

[Gathered together, fear and prey forgot; Supported by a thronging choir it flew. A joyous multitude with pious gifts Followed its flight.][57]

Although in the Old English poem no mention is made of giftgiving, the description of the jewel-like beauty of the reborn bird and the indication that its appearance is commemorated in books and marble is followed, as in the Latin poem, by reverential worship:

>   . . . Ðonne fugla cynn
> on healfa gehwōre   hēapum þringað,
> sigað sīdwegum,   songe lofiað
> mærað mōdigne   meaglum reordum
> ond swā þone hālgan   hringe beteldað
> flyhte on lyfte; . . . .
>
> (335–40)

[Then all about him   the race of birds
In flocks assemble   on every side,
Winging from far ways,   singing his praises,
Hymning their hero   in fervent strains;
Around the Phoenix   in circling flight
They attend the holy one   high in air.]

These scenes of worship contain, I think, traces of the practice of exhibiting girls who have completed the process of female initiation. The manifestation of these girls to their community is considered a sacred rite; they are made the object of songs and gifts. In his study of patterns of religious initiation, *Rites and Symbols of Initiation*, Eliade comments apropos of the solemn manifestation of initiated girls: "It is a ceremonial announcement that the mystery has been accomplished. The girl is *shown* to be adult, that is, to be ready to assume the mode of being proper to woman. To show something ceremonially—a sign, an object, an animal, a man—is to declare a sacred presence, to acclaim the miracle of hierophany."[58] Considered in these terms the scene of manifestation is out of place in both poems: the context in each is that of birth, not menarche, for the phoenix that is worshipped is the offspring of the original bird.

If my speculation is correct and the scene of manifestation—as well as other details drawn from menarche ritual—is misplaced in the Birth Sequence, the scene is as "misplaced" in Lactantius's birth section as it is in that of the Anglo-Saxon poet. Yet we cannot in the case of the Latin poem appeal for an explanation to the misplacing of a formulaic pattern through oral composition. No one has ever suggested that the African poet's *Carmen* is anything but a literary creation, and I do not propose to here. There is, however, apart from genesis in oral composition, one other possible explanation for the overlapping of details drawn from menstrual and birth ritual that appear in the Latin and Old English poems. Perhaps the ritual behavior that lies in the background of the poem's action was not itself always so distinctly divided into "menstrual" and "birth" ceremonies. J. M. Winterbottom, in his account of the Cewa tribe of Zambia, stresses that the whole process of initiation, beginning with "the little initiation" at puberty and ending with "the great initiation" after the girl is pregnant, must really be thought of as one rite, each stage of which is part of a continuous celebration of the flowering of fertility.[59]

But we are still left with the problem of the escort. The Anglo-Saxon poet, apart from details he inherited from Lactantius's poem, could not very likely have had independent knowledge of the escorts who play a role in African female initiation ceremonies. Where did the detail come from? Blake notes in the introduction to his edition of *The Phoenix* that "the first classical author to mention that the phoenix is accompanied by a crowd of birds is Tacitus."[60] But when one looks at the passage in Tacitus it seems clear that the crowd referred to is the one that praises the reborn bird on its return to Heliopolis, not the one the Anglo-Saxon poet has given the old phoenix to attend its journey into the waste:

> As to its term of years, the tradition varies. The generally received number is five hundred; but there are some who assert that its visits fall at intervals of 1461 years, and that it was in the reigns first of Sesosis, then Amasis, and finally of Ptolemy . . . that the three earlier phoenixes flew to the city called Heliopolis with a great escort of common birds amazed at the novelty of their appearance.[61]

The common birds are gazing at the phoenix in its renewed glory. Ronald Syme, in his magisterial study of Tacitus, takes Tacitus's reference to Heliopolis to mark the return journey, not the going out: "Tacitus goes on to recount in poetic language the demise of the phoenix: the bird renewed, rising from the nest and dutifully transporting the remains of his parent to the temple of the Sun."[62]

In sum, we are still left with the question Cross raises—"why the retinue of birds on the way to Syria . . ."?[63] All that can be said, finally, is that the Anglo-Saxon poet hit on a detail—perhaps, through a mistaken interpretation of the passage in Tacitus—that fits the gynecological context of the rest of the images in the inherited sequence of images and actions.

As we shall see in our discussion of the effect of this gynecological background on the allegorical meaning of the Christian Old English poem, the imaginative use of material enlarges its range of reference; it is revalorized within a Christian allegorical framework. Thus, for example, the worshippers of the jewel-like phoenix, considered from the perspective of Christian allegory—the perspective of chapter 5—may be readily identified as the host of angels who attend the two major events of Christ's life: the Resurrection and, perhaps even more important, now that we understand how the gynecological material pervades the text, the Nativity. Furthermore, we may begin to approach, perhaps more successfully than we could the question of the escort, three other problems underscored by Cross: (1) why the application of an epithet meaning " 'gray feathered' to a bird that is later portrayed in bright and startling color?"[64] (2) why the intermediate stage in the wilderness before the journey to Syria? and (3) why the apparent "second thousand year cycle for the reborn Phoenix"?[65]

Fertility is the central idea implicit in the entire range of those aspects of the history of embryology and anthropology with which I have attempted to unlock a heretofore hidden dimension of the poems' symbolism. The central symbols of the poems contain the obvious foundation for transformation into Christian allegory, most especially the phoenix's fountain, so easily convertible to the *fons vitae*, variously interpreted by the church fathers as Christ—especially as he is contemplated in his death and Resurrection—baptism, Mater Ecclesia, the womb of Mary, the Evangelists, and Holy Scripture. The Anglo-Saxon poet's treatment of the Latin poem is, indeed, a testament to how tempting it could be to revalorize the images of the pagan poem. Even so, as we shall see in the following chapter, the feminine range of meaning pushes its way to the surface.

5

A REEXAMINATION OF THE MEANING
OF *THE PHOENIX*

It is to be expected that the feminine content of the cultural and scientific influences, having entered the Old English poem through the imagery borrowed from Lactantius, will have become manifest, as well as transformed, once this imagery is pressed into so defined a Christian allegorical framework as we have in the Old English *Phoenix*, and it does. The emergence and transformation of this feminine dimension requires interpretation by the critical reader. In this chapter I propose to demonstrate that when pressured by its placement within an allegorical context, the feminine dimension of Lactantius's predominantly pagan poem is so jostled that *sub rosa*, as it were, Mariology invades Christology. The phoenix in the garden near the fountain that overflows twelve times yearly may be interpreted as a symbol of the Virgin Mary as well as of the maternity of the Church, and the theme of Incarnation may be seen to move together with that of Resurrection in the drama of salvation. On one level *The Phoenix* deals with the growing up of Mary and—when the phoenix's birth cycle repeats itself—the coming to perfection of the good Christian. Like the female initiate prohibited from touching ground, the phoenix perched in the tree will achieve a new status: it will move from being the Virgin in the garden to becoming Mother of God. As in the initiation ritual of young African girls, transformation is at the center of what happens to the phoenix. Its movement toward conception makes possible its own renewal and, as an embodiment of Mary (and the Church), that of all humanity.

To be sure, objections to such an interpretation might be raised. It would be legitimate to point out, for example, that if such a level were present in the poem, the Anglo-Saxon poet would surely have told us about it in his homiletic commentary. But, in fact, what we find in the homiletic second half of *The Phoenix* as an allegorical interpretation of its preceding 380 lines, the paraphrase of Lactantius's *Carmen de Ave Phoenice*, is essentially Christological: the reborn phoenix is the risen Christ as well as the redeemed good Christian whose redemption the Resurrection makes possible. Robert Burlin has been content to find the "flexibility" of the phoenix symbol in this straightforward, Christ-good Christian duality.[1] Burlin's adherence to the reading of the homiletic commentary notwithstanding, I think that, on closer scrutiny, the phoenix symbol proves to have even more radiance: it is a *double* dual image. The absence of explicit discussion of a Marian dimension in the poem need mean neither that the Anglo-Saxon poet did not intend to make it part of the poem's structure nor that he was unaware of the possibilities of such a level of interpretation. There is evidence, as I hope to demonstrate in this chapter, that some of the Anglo-Saxon poet's additions to and recrafting of the imagery are motivated by an intention to develop the Marian potential of the symbolism. My exploration of this dimension of the poem is not intended to stand as *the* interpretation, supplanting currently held scholarly opinion; I am merely following one of two parallel lines in the poem: Mary and Christ, Incarnation and Resurrection, coordinates in the drama of salvation. This chapter is offered as a contribution toward a more complete understanding the *The Phoenix* and as a reading that suggests a larger role for Mary in early medieval thought than is usually claimed for her.

Another objection to seeing a feminine fold in the allegory not only *might* be raised but *was*, by a friend and fellow medievalist: if there is a feminine dimension to the phoenix symbol, why does the poet not use the feminine pronoun in referring to the bird? My response was—and is—because it would be an unnecessary clarification, although there is a precedent for using the feminine gender in the pre-Christian poet Laevius.[2] The indeterminate gender of the phoenix—" . . . God āna wāt, / Cyning ælmihtig   hū his gecynde bið, / wīfhādes þe weres; . . ." (355–57, "God only knows, / The Almighty King, what his breed may be, / Or male or female; . . ."—operates like the androgynous nature of the Neolithic Bird Goddesses that, far from excluding the creative potential of the female, includes that of the male, thereby exemplifying Eliade's idea that creation "springs from an over-fullness, from a wholeness."[3] If we must move back in time from the phoenix for the analogy of the Bird Goddesses, we must move forward in time for my next analogy to the phoenix's androgynous wholeness: the Church. Speaking of the nuptial relationship between Christ and the Church, Augustine observes that the Apostle Paul speaks of the Church as a maiden (2 Corinthians 112) even though Paul is "addressing so many persons of both sexes including not only youths and maidens but also married men and women."[4] This analogy has particular relevance to my examination in view of the relationship I perceive between the phoenix and Mary and her position as archetype of the Church.

Historically, the Fathers and Doctors of the Church have made the phoenix do double duty. While St. Clement of Rome (*Epistle to the*

Corinthians 1.25), Tertullian (*De Resurrectione Carnis* 13), and St. Cyril (*Cathechesis* 18), among others, concentrate on the phoenix's resemblance to the risen Christ, Rufinus and Albertus Magnus put the emphasis on Mary by stressing that the phoenix conceives alone. The early church father Rufinus, in his *Commentarius in Symbolum Apostolorum*, refers to the phoenix in a question apropos of Mary's virginal conception:

> But what is remarkable about the conception by a virgin when that eastern bird which they call the phoenix is likewise born without a spouse . . . ?[5]

Pointing to Albertus Magnus's comparison of Mary to the phoenix *quae est unica avis sine patre* ("which is a unique bird without a father"), Beryl Rowland, in her study of bird imagery, *Birds with Human Souls*, observes of the phoenix that some "writers stressed the bird's uniqueness, solitariness, its sinless self-reproduction, and found the bird a suitable symbol for the Virgin herself."[6] Thus, the early history of the phoenix's use as a Christian symbol anticipates Donne's later allusion to the phoenix in *The Canonization*: ". . . to one neutral thing both sexes fit."[7] Modern scholarship has tended to be Christological in its reading of the Old English *Phoenix*. To the extent that Burlin (32–33) sees the duality of the phoenix symbol as consisting in a relationship between the phoenix and Christ and between the phoenix and the good Christian, he is in general agreement with the current interpretation of what the phoenix represents.[8] Without denying that these connections exist, I propose to reexamine, in this chapter, some of the images central to the three broad movements of the first half of the poem in the context of scriptural and patristic writings relevant to the Virgin Mary and to the concept of Mater Ecclesia.

The Virgin in the Garden

An understanding of how the images of the garden and some of its constituent parts (i.e., the fountain, the gate) function as aspects of the feminine dimension of the poem is critical to the full appreciation of *The Phoenix*. If there can be any doubt about the identity of the phoenix's home far in the East, which is described in the first eighty-four lines of *The Phoenix*, that doubt is dispelled in the homiletic second half of the poem. The phoenix's garden is the same place God created for Adam and Eve:

> Habbaþ wē geascad   þæt se Ælmihtiga
> worhte wer ond wīf   þurh his wundra spēd
> ond hī þā gesette   on þone sēlestan
> foldan sceates,   þone fira bearn

nemnað neorxnawong,   þær him nænges wæs
ēades onsȳn,   þenden Ēces word,
Hālges hlēoþorcwide   healdan woldan
on þām nīwan gefēan. . . .

(393–400)

[We have learned that our Maker   in fullness of might
Shaped man and woman,   and set their home
In the winsomest region   of all the world,
Paradise named   and known among men.
In their new-born bliss   they lacked no blessing
As long as they heeded   the Holy One's word,
Their Maker's command. . . .]

After their disobedience, the earthly paradise was "fæste bitȳned" (419, "bolted fast") until "His hidercyme" (421, his[Christ's] advent).

But, of course, the reader does not really need this explanation. Putting aside for the moment the question of how the phoenix came to be sole occupant of "se foldan scēat / ofer middangeard" (3–4, "that far-off realm") that "āfyrred is / þurh Meotudes meaht   mānfremmendum" (5–6, "[Is] set apart from the sinful by the power of God"), let us reconsider the description of Eden with which *The Phoenix* begins.

The primary impression that the vision of Eden creates is that it is a beautiful place: *þæt torhte lond* (28, "that lovely land"). It is radiant with joy and sweet fragrance: "Wlitig is se wong eall,   wynnum geblissad / mid þām fægrestum   foldan stencum (7–8, "Beauteous that country and blessed with joys, / With the fairest odours of all the earth"). Music from the heavenly choir fills the air: "Ðær bið oft open, ēadgum tōgeanes / onhliden hlēoþra wyn, heofonrīces duru" (11–12, "There ever stand open the portals of heaven / With songs of rapture for blessed souls"). The landscape is smooth and unmarred by cliffs, gorges, caves or crags (21–26), and the land is blessed with a temperate, sunny climate (14–19). Of all the qualities that compose the beauty of this terrestrial paradise, the most emphasized is its fruitfulness: "Is þæt æþele lond / blōstmum geblōwen" (20–21, "The lovely land / Is rich with blossoms"). Leaves never wither on eternally green trees (38–39), the woods are in blossom summer and winter (37–38), and fruits hang ripe in all seasons (74–77). Fecund wells and streams nurture the garden:

. . . lagustrēamas,
wundrum wrǣtlice   wyllan onspringað
fægrum flodwylmum . . . .

(62–64)

[. . . running streams
And welling waters   wondrously spring
Overflowing earth   from fountains fair.]

Arguing persuasively that the "vision of paradise in *The Phoenix* . . . forms the *locus* from which we can derive the meaning of the poem," Calder points out that for one major scholar the dominant note struck in patristic writings on paradise is "the beauty of Eden."[9] Following this clue into his own examination of *The Phoenix*, Calder concludes that the poem "is a rendering of the relationship between beauty and salvation" and that "the poet creates a paradise that attracts man through its beauty to participate in an activity that imitates the art of God."[10] While Calder heads in the right direction, his decision to avoid treating the poem as "a formal Christian allegory" makes him seek out an idea general enough to unite "all differing allegorical perspectives in one symbolic vision."[11]

About the nature of the garden's beauty we can be more specific: it is a feminine reflection. Within the Christian frame established by the Old English poet, the reflection can be identified with two mothers: one responsible for bearing the son of God on earth, the Virgin Mary, and the other for perpetuating the redemptive process that sprang out of Christ, that is, Mater Ecclesia or the Church. Given Lactantius's eventual development into one of the African church fathers of the fourth century—whether or not he wrote the source of the first half of the Old English poem before his conversion to Christianity[12]—it is worth noting that the great Jesuit theologian, Jean Daniélou, has observed that "the idea of the maternity of the Church . . . seems to have been developed especially in Africa."[13] And a common figure for Mater Ecclesia was the paradisial garden. The key figures in the early African Church were Latinized Phoenicians and Roman settlers; Lactantius belonged to the latter group. Most of the African Fathers, even the Phoenicians among them who came from a maritime tradition, were either close to the soil themselves or close to those who were tillers of the fields. Thus, they inherited the habit of drawing analogies between the "fertility of the soil and that of woman," a habit that E. O. James has called "one of the salient features in agricultural society of all times."[14] To cite just two representative examples, we find, for instance, in St. Cyprian, Bishop of Carthage (executed in A.D. 248), a description of the Church, regarded as feminine, in terms of the earthly paradise, full of the same trees and waters encountered in the garden of *The Phoenix*. He writes, "The Church, like Paradise, includes fruit-bearing trees within her walls. . . . She waters the trees from four rivers, which are the four gospels."[15] Likewise, Origen (A.D. 185–253), an African church father from Alexandria, conceives of the Church in terms of paradise: "Those who are born again in baptism are placed in Paradise, that is, in the Church."[16] In Augustine, Bishop of Hippo, the development of the early African Church reaches its culmination, and a student of his Mariology has called the Mary-Ecclesia parallel one of Augustine's favorite ideas.[17]

Here, a line from his *Sermon 188,* on the Nativity, may serve as an illustration: "The holy Church, as a virgin, celebrates today the Child-bearing of a virgin."[18] From the perspective of the conception of Mary as an archetype of the Church and the relationship between the garden image and the archetype, a reading used at the Mass of the Immaculate Conception is illuminating:

> From eternity, in the beginning, he created me,
>   and for eternity I shall remain. . . .
> I have grown tall as a cedar on Lebanon,
>   as a cypress on Mount Hermon;
> I have grown tall as a palm in Engedi,
>   as the rose bushes of Jericho;
>   as a fine olive in the plain,
>   as a plane tree I have grown tall.
> I have exhaled a perfume like cinnamon and acacia,
> I have breathed out a scent like choice myrrh, ...
>   (Ecclesiasticus 24:9–20)

Presumably the Church—and, therefore, Mary as archetype of the Church—here sees her origins in her relationship to Wisdom before the Creation.[19] The evocation in Ecclesiasticus of the lush, watered garden filled with all manner of tall trees and redolent with fragrance clearly resembles the phoenix's home. Indeed, the sources of the sweet scents— cinnamon and balm, especially—are among those that are closely associated with the birth of the young phoenix in the Latin poem (83–84).

Although the feast of the Immaculate Conception appeared in England in the twelfth century, the reading from Ecclesiasticus did not become part of the Mass until 1476, when Pope Sixtus IV ordered the composition of a new formulary for the Mass of the Immaculate Conception.[20] The relationship of Mary to the paradisial garden, however, echoed in the reading from Ecclesiasticus, is articulated by the earliest Fathers of the Church. A typical example, cited by Thomas Livius in his pioneering study, *The Blessed Virgin in the Fathers of the First Six Centuries,* comes from St. Ephrem's exegesis of Genesis 1:26–28:

> O Mary, most holy paradise in Eden, bearing fruit most beautiful and most pleasant. . . . Rejoice, O Virgin maid, thou tree of goodly foliage, whence we gather the fruit, of which when we eat we are refreshed with gladness and do not die. . . . Hail, paradise of delights; hail tree of life; hail, fountain of grace and immortality. . . .[21]

At the center of the garden in the Old English poem is the fountain that overflows twelve times annually; it is the source of creativity at the heart of the Mary-Ecclesia parallel. The overflowing fountain stands in obviously antithetical relationship to the destructive waters of Noah's Flood alluded to early in the poem as having left the phoenix's garden unscathed:

> . . . Swā iū wætres þrym
> ealne middangeard,   mereflōd þeahte,
> eorþan ymbhwyrft,   þā se æþla wong
> æghwæs onsund   wið yðfare
> gehealden stōd   hrēora wǣga
> ēadig unwemme   þurh ēst Godes,
>
>   (41–46)

> [. . . As the waters of old,
> The sea-floods, covered   the compass of earth
> And the pleasant plain   stood all uninjured,
> By the grace of God   unhurt and unharmed.]

Though it is *þēodnes gebod* (68, "God's bidding") that causes the waters of the fountain to overflow the land twelve times a year, the fountain, as I tried to demonstrate in chapter 2, owes a debt to human physiology. In an unpublished doctoral dissertation, Thomas Smith pointed to the fountain as a puzzle in the garden landscape. While praising the opening description as one of the finest representations of the traditional paradisial gardens of the patristic commentaries, he noted: "The flooding of the garden clearly involves a yearly cycle, which is a significant departure from the ancient tradition of the earthly paradise."[22] The difference derives, I think, from Lactantius's knowledge of the initiation ceremonies discussed in the preceding chapters; these ceremonies must have been even longer and more evident in the Africa of his day than in our own. When the English poet takes Lactantius's image up and places it within an obviously Christian allegorical context, it is unmistakably transformed into a religious symbol. Moreover, it is particularly accessible to interpretation by the church fathers of Africa and Asia Minor (in close commercial contact with the northern and eastern coasts of Africa during the early centuries of the Church). They are fond of the notion of the motherhood of the Church because they are conditioned by the same elemental forces at work in the imagination of Lactantius. Thus, if St. Methodius, who St. Jerome alleges was Bishop of Tyre during the third century,[23] were asked to interpret the phoenix's bathing twelve times in the fountain that overflows as often, he might have offered the following explanation, couched in terms of the womb of Mother Church:

> For just as a woman receives the unformed seed of her husband and after a period of time brings forth a perfect human being, so too the

Church one might say, constantly conceiving those who take refuge in the Word, and shaping them according to the likeness and form of Christ, after a certain time makes them citizens of that blessed age. Hence, it is necessary that she should stand upon the laver as the mother of those who are washed. So, too, the function she exercises over the laver is called the moon.[24]

First, it should be observed that the phoenix stands where the Church should be: on the fountain. Second, the process described in St. Methodius's passage can begin only after Mary has given birth to Christ, the germ of the Church. As it happens, St. Methodius is here offering comment on chapter 12 of The Apocalypse, specifically on the woman clothed with the sun, a figure of the Church, who labors to give birth to her children. We will turn to this scriptural passage when we reconsider the Birth Sequence from the perspective of Christian allegory. But it is clear, at this point, that before the womb of the Church can give birth to its members, the womb of Mary must first have conceived at the Incarnation. The phoenix at the fountain, therefore, is simultaneously Mary awaiting the fulfillment of the Annunciation and Mother Church yielding grace that will unfold in time and space to her members. In other words, until the cycle begins with the first phoenix, the process cannot perpetuate itself. In light of my contention that gynecological imagery in *The Phoenix* complements Christian imagery, David Jeffrey's analysis of the frontispiece ("Alpha and Omega," Bib. Nat. M.S. Lat. 9438) to his book, *By Things Seen*, is of interest.[25] The illumination pictures Christ seated in a mandorla that contains two interlocking circles. Jeffrey comments that the circles are "symbolic of the two realms, uncreated and created, eternal and temporal, which cohere in him [Christ]. . . . The vaginal shape of the mandorla itself may," he continues, "not unfairly be related to the subject, which as Bonaventure puts it, for example, in his *Reductione artium ad theologiam*, is 'the eternal incarnation of the Son of God.' "[26] Having already approached the fountain earlier in this study as an aspect of what I called the Menstrual Sequence, I would like to call attention to the following passage, which appears in Hugo Rahner's survey of the figure of the moon in patristic literature. According to traditional exegesis, the moon that is the Church is the source of baptismal waters:

> Wie Selene in der Kraft der im Synodos mit Helios erlebten Vernichtung zur Mutter der lebendigen Dinge auf Erden, zur gnadenmilden Spenderin des fruchtzeugenden Mondewassers zum nächtlichen Quell des Taues wird, so erhält die in Christus hineinsterbende Kirche gerade in der täglichen Vernichtung ihrer irdischen Sichtbarkeit, in der mystischen Finsternis ihrer Vereinigung mit Christus die Kraft zur Zeugung geistlichen Lebens,

wird zum Quell des geistträchtigen Taufwassers, zur Spenderin des Taues der Gnade, den sie im nächtlichen Schweigen dieser irdischen Leben ausgiesst. Sie führt so die Kinder, die sie geboren hat, hinauf zur seligen Freiheit in den reinen, ätherfeuchtenden Gefilde, die über dem Mond sind, macht sie frei von aller unter dem Mond herrschenden damonischen Gebundheit.[27]

[Just as Selene, the Moon, in virtue of the annihilation she suffers in the course of her intercourse with Helios, the Sun, becomes the mother of the living things on earth, the gentle giver of the fertilising moon waters, and the nightly wellspring of dews, so the Church, dying in Christ, preserves the power to procreate spiritual lives precisely in the daily annihilation of her temporal invisibility in the mystical darkness of her union with Christ, and becomes the fountain of spiritually pregnant baptismal waters and giver of dews of grace which she pours out in the nightlike silence of this earthly life. Thus she leads the children she has borne from here to the blissful freedom in the pure Elysian fields above the moon and sets them free of all the demonic bondage that prevails under the moon.]

Although the passage is baroque in its periodicity, I have quoted it in full because of the clear equation it draws between the Church and the moon goddess, Selene, and between the baptismal waters and the fertilizing moon waters (which would seem to be a reference to the catamenia). Both fecund waters are described as having their source in a female figure. In light of the menstrual association of the phoenix fountain discussed in chapter 2 and the relationship I shall be developing here between the phoenix and Mary, archetype of the Church, Rahner's passage seems to be a ratification of my own insights. Mary is herself as frequently linked to the fountain in the garden of Eden as is the Church. Albertus Magnus, to cite an example that is comparatively late in a long tradition, writes that Mary is the fountain of ablution referred to in Zechariah 13 ("When that day comes, a fountain will be opened for the House of David and the citizens of Jerusalem, for sin and impurity"). He also links her to Canticles 4: "Fountain of the garden, well of living waters. She is the fountain in respect to the common benefits which she displays to all men, and the well in respect to the deep and spiritual devotion she offers to her devotees."[28]

Perhaps more explicit than the fountain as a clue to Mary's presence is the image of the gate in the garden "feor heonan / ēastdǣlum" (1–2, "far to the eastward"): "Ðǣr bið oft open, . . . heofonrīces duru" (11–12, "There ever stand open the portals of heaven." In the same work in which Rufinus discusses the phoenix as a symbol of the virginity of Mary, he observes that Ezekiel calls Mary "The gate of the Lord,"

meaning that through her the Lord entered the world. Thus he says: "But the gate which looks towards the East shall be shut, and shall not be opened, and no one shall pass through it; for the Lord God of Israel shall pass through it, and it shall be shut." [44:2]. Could a more explicit hint have been given of the Virgin's being kept inviolate? The gate which was shut was her virginity. Through it the Lord God of Israel entered; through it He advanced into this world from the Virgin's womb.[29]

The gate (or door) image is a favorite one of the church fathers and in their hands it underwent many metamorphoses. For instance, in one of Augustine's Nativity sermons, the doors first close on Christ's tomb, then transform themselves into doors on a church wherein the risen Christ is manifest to its members, and finally they become the familiar doors to the womb of Mary:

> Though the doors of the house were closed, He manifested His mature body to those within the house, and . . . as an infant He came forth, a spouse from His bride-chamber, that is from the virginal womb.[30]

In St. Ambrose's handling of the door image in a letter from the Synod of Milan in 390, we have an explanation of what the closed doors of Mary have to do with the open doors to heaven in the phoenix's eastern garden. Ambrose writes,

> But what is that gate to the sanctuary, that external gate on the East, which remains closed? *No one*, it is said, *shall pass through it except only the God of Israel* (Ezech. XLIV, 2). Is not this gate Mary, through whom the Redeemer entered the world? . . . . This gate is the blessed Mary, about whom it is written: *the Lord shall pass through it, and it will remain closed* (Ezech. XLIV, 2) after birth, for it was a virgin who conceived and brought forth.[31]

In other words, by miraculously bearing the Word made flesh through her closed gate, Mary opens the closed gate of heaven. This is the door that *The Phoenix* poet writes "bið oft open" (11). The door was closed by Eve, one of the first two inhabitants of the garden in the east. Albertus Magnus would have it that Eve is the western whereas Mary is the eastern gate:

> Mary is aptly called the Eastern Gate: because through her the true Orient entered the world, he who visited us from on high: and because through her grace has risen in us, and access is provided to the true Orient, namely Christ, who arose from her: she is the principle of our ascent to life. The western gate was Eve, who was the principle of our approach to the fall and to death.[32]

Thus the evocation of the Virgin Mary and the Church, of which she is the archetype, plays in the opening description of the garden, against the explanation of how it was lost through Eve in lines 393ff., quoted at the beginning of this section.

We come now to the question we put aside earlier—that of how the phoenix came to be the sole occupant of the garden. If the reader sees the opening sequence of the poem as the *start* of a cycle that will repeat itself after the conclusion of the Birth Sequence, he must see the phoenix in this first instance as a symbol of Mary in all her purity, predestined to bear Christ. There is no more fitting locus for her wait than Eden, scene of the original innocence as well as of the Fall, from whose consequences she will cooperate in saving humankind. Until Mary bears Christ there can be no other inhabitants of Eden. To repeat the line from Ecclesiasticus quoted earlier, it can be said of the phoenix that it is created immaculate "from eternity in the beginning" like Mary. The phoenix inhabits the paradisial garden because from the moment it came into being, it was oriented toward the God of the East. Further, because the phoenix is, from the first moment, free from original sin, it may also serve to embody the Church whose essence is existence in Christ as his Mystical Body. The early Fathers saw Mary as a second Eve whose divine maternity was the foundation of her grace. Augustine writes of her immaculate conception:

> Of the holy Virgin Mary, in whose case, out of respect for the Lord, I would have no question raised when there is talk of sin—for how do we know what further grace was conferred on her for absolute victory over sin, she who deserved to conceive and bear Him who obviously had no sin?[33]

A similar passage appears in Ambrose who attributes her fullness of grace to the divine maternity:

> For Mary alone was this greeting [full of grace] reserved; for she is well said to be alone full of grace, who alone obtained the grace which no one else had gained, to be filled with the author of grace.[34]

Finally, to cite one last example, Zeno of Verona likewise says Mary deserved to bear Christ because she was born holy in body and spirit.[35] Mary's incorrupt fecundity is embodied in the luxuriant vegetation of the phoenix's garden. When the bird flies up to the "heanne beam" at line 112 to await the sun, its fulfillment is at hand. Indeed, there may be evidence that the figure of the phoenix poised in the branches of the tree adumbrates the foundation of the Church through the coming birth of Christ (the young phoenix). In his study, *Early Christian Symbolism in Great Britain and Ireland*, J. Romilly Allen describes two very similar designs that decorate the vaulted roofs of the apses of two early churches: the Church of SS. Cosmas and Damian (A.D. 526–30) and the Church of St. Praxede (A.D. 820). Both are in Rome, the former having been built by Pope Felix IV and the latter rebuilt by Pope Paschal I. What strikes one about Allen's long detailed descriptions of the designs over the apses is this: in both designs there is a palm tree with a phoenix in its branches immediately behind the figure identified as the founder of the church. In the Church of SS. Cosmas and Damian, the phoenix perches in a palm behind Pope Felix who holds a model of his church,[36] and in the case of the Church of St. Praxede the same tree-phoenix combination appears behind Pope Paschal, who carries a model of his church.[37] Although Allen's object is simply to describe all the parallel figures of these two designs, it is possible, nonetheless, to infer from the combination that I note that the palm-phoenix motif has iconographic significance as a type of the Church. If such is the case, the phoenix's movement from the active water play in the fountain to the static wait in the high tree, punctuating clearly the end of the first sequence of the poem by the shift from action to inaction, offers an even more emphatic conclusion, for it clearly foreshadows the events about to unfold in the Conception and Birth Sequences that follow.

J. B. Mayor discusses the Church of St. Praxede as marking the increased importance of Mary in the art of the early Middle Ages.[38] The church is one of two built by Pope Paschal I in the ninth century that represent Mary enthroned as the Queen of Heaven at the center of their apses. Thus, well before manifestations of popular devotion to Mary in the twelfth and thirteenth centuries, we see her usurping Christ's traditional position in the apse of the church. Mary has the same position in the mosaic decorating the apse of an even earlier church: the sixth-century cathedral of Parenzo in Istria. Also, in sixth-century paintings depicting Mary with Jesus and the Apostles, haloes give special status to both Jesus and his mother, while the Apostles, shown without haloes, clearly have a lower status.

Instances of Mary's prominence in early medieval art are paralleled by signs of service to Mary among religious thinkers. It was common since Augustine's time for ecclesiastics to identify themselves as *servi Dei* but awareness is growing of a notion of service to Mary in monastic writers such as Odilo of Cluny, Anselm of Canterbury, Eadmer of Canterbury, Bernard of Clairvaux and Aelrod of Rievaulx.[39] Jotsaldus, a biographer and disciple of Odilo of Cluny (962–1049), styles his master a "Servant of St. Mary" and Odilo himself is author of a hymn on the assumption (*Hymnus in Assumptione*) in which he calls Mary *regina*, glorious above all creation, and the singers of her praises, *supplices*, a position associated with service.[40] Similar expressions of service to Mary are found in prayers written in her honor by Anselm of Canterbury (1033–1109).

Anselm views Mary as having dominion and as being worthy of service because of her divine maternity, her collaboration in the work of redemption, and her role as intercessor for humanity with God.[41] The Marian dimension that I am pointing to, then, in the Old English *Phoenix* is not an isolated instance of Marian piety in the early Middle Ages.

Conception

As the phoenix flies up from its tree to meet the rising sun, a traditional sign of Christ, at lines 120–24, the Conception—or, in specifically Marian terms, the Annunciation—Sequence begins. The flight upward to the sun may remind the reader of the question from Canticles 6:10, "Who is this arising like the dawn. . . ?" and the suggestion here of the Bride of Canticles is appropriate, for she has consistently been interpreted in Christian times as the Church, Christ's Bride, of whom the Virgin is the prime type by virtue of her most intimate union with Christ in the drama of salvation. That drama commenced when Mary, with her obedient, "I am the handmaid of the Lord" (Luke 1:38), accepted the angel's invitation to "Rejoice" (Luke 1:28) and put herself at God's disposal for the accomplishment of his designs. The phoenix has waited in patient inaction for this moment and its soaring flight upward is in strong contrast to its former inactivity, reflecting, perhaps, a deliberate act of will congruent with Mary's receptivity. Certainly the phoenix's meeting with the sun is marked by *joyfulness:* it sings melodiously in flight (124) and its heart is filled with bliss (126). There is the sense that something wondrous has happened; no sound since the world was created can compare to the phoenix's song (127–31). The joyfulness of the bird involves the world, for we are told that of all the things God gave to relieve man's cares in this world, nothing is so remarkable as the phoenix's song:

> ne magon þām breahtme   bȳman ne hornas
> ne hearpan hlyn   ne hæleþa stefn
> ænges on eorþan   ne organan,
> swēglēoþres geswin   ne swanes feðre
> ne ænig þāra drēama   þe Dryhten gescōp
> gumum tō glīwe   in þās gēomran woruld.
>
> (134–39)

> [. . . Neither trumpet nor horn,
> Nor melody of harp   is like to that lay,
> Nor voice of man,   nor strain of organ music,
> Nor swan's singing feathers,   nor any pleasant sound
> That God gave for joy to men   in this mournful world.]

The quintessence of human joy is identified in the second half of *The Phoenix* with the Advent of Christ (421) who comes to rescue man from this "geomran woruld" (139, mournful world). I would suggest that the phoenix's wondrous song can be seen as a celebration of that moment when, according to Luke 1:35, the power of the Holy Spirit covered the Virgin "with its shadow." It may be too much to suggest here that the Old English poet has made the phoenix, who is resplendent with color in all other sections of the poem, "se haswa fugel" (121, "The gray bird"), as it seeks the sun, because of the Holy Spirit's *overshadowing*. Nonetheless, it should be pointed out that the idea of "shadow" does appear twice again: immediately before the young phoenix's birth when the phoenix is said to make its home in shadow: "in scade weardað" (168) and then soon afterwards when the growing young bird is described as developing "on sceade" (234).

The cause-and-effect relationship between the phoenix's song and the bird's union with the rising sun is as strong in the poem by Lactantius as in *The Phoenix:*

> atque ubi Sol pepulit fulgentis limina portae
> et primi emicuit luminis aura levis,
> incipit illa sacri modulamina fundere cantus
>
> (43–45)

> [And when the sun has knocked at the threshold of the shining gate and the faint gleam of the first light has darted forth, she begins to pour forth the notes of a holy chant.]

Those scholars who judge the *Carmen de Ave Phoenice* to be early Christian rather than pagan might see here evidence of the Marian "gate of the Lord figure" and a suggestion of the descent of the Logos into the womb of Mary. Despite the description of the phoenix's song as sacred, however, the proper analogue for the Lactantian gate is, I think, another, which we encountered in chapter 3: the door praised in the female initiation ceremony. It is clear from the song that opens the rite of the Chaga that to them the door is "sacred":

> "Who was it who put the door there?". . . . It is the Chief! It is the Great God! It is he who made the door through which everyone has to pass!

Lactantius's gate is *sacred* to the same extent. Although the song's appearance in the midst of such classical references as those to Phoebus (41), the Cyllenean lyre (50), and Olympian fields (41) does not in itself rule out the possibility of a Christian range of reference, the absence of a sharply defined Christian framework such as is developed in the Old English poem keeps from the Latin poem the necessary catalyst for transforming borrowed images from rites, treatments, and ideas about menarche and birth into Christian figures.

The reference to God's creation of the world in lines 129–31 of the Anglo-Saxon poem reminds us that what is happening to the phoenix is part of a generative process reaching into eternity. In the beginning God took dust from the virgin earth and, without seed, created Adam. Now in the virgin phoenix, a symbol of Mary, he fashions the New Adam, Christ. The new phoenix is destined to return to the garden, an equivalent of the Church, and repeat the process. Speaking to the members of the Church one Christmas Day, Augustine exhorts them to imitate Mary:

> Do, in the inner chambers of your soul, what you view with amazement in the flesh of Mary. He who believes in his heart unto justice conceives Christ.[42]

St. Methodius, too, views the Incarnation as the beginning of a circular process within the body of the Church. He writes that the newly formed Christian

> is brought forth as by mothers in labor by those who are more perfect, until they are born and reborn unto the greatness and beauty of virtue. And when by their progress these too have become the Church, they cooperate in their turn in the birth and rearing of other children, bringing to term in the receptive soul as in a mother's womb, the spotless desire of the Word.[43]

The Old English poet seems to be aware of this process. Cross points out that, while "Lactantius makes no mention of a second cycle of life" in the English poem, "there appears to be a second thousand-year cycle for the reborn Phoenix if *eft* 'again' (366 b) has real meaning, as it seems to in the context."[44] For Cross the idea of a second cycle savors of "the Stoic belief in cyclic conflagrations,"[45] but the preceding passages from Augustine and Methodius may serve to remind us that there is a cyclic process in the body of the Church that well suits the poets' Christian conception of the poem.

The phoenix, therefore, joined to the light that descends from the Father is at once the Virgin Mary and Mother Church. At the end of the Conception Sequence the phoenix leaves the earthly paradise and enters the waste of this world, a movement that earlier was discussed as a reflection of the primitive practice of bearing children in seclusion. It will be recalled that whereas the phoenix of the Latin poem seeks out Syria, its counterpart in the Old English poem makes a two-stage journey, going first to the desert and then to the "Sywara lond" (166). From a Marian perspective, the fact that the Old English poet has added a stop may be significant. The Gospel informs us that after the Annunciation, Mary went to stay with her relative, Elizabeth, who lived in a town in the hills of Judaea; she stayed three months (Luke 1:56). The Old English poet may have added the phoenix's stop in the "wēsten" (161, "waste") where it resides for a "þrāge" (161, "season") to reinforce the Marian dimension of the phoenix symbol. As for the phoenix's subsequent departure for Syria, that location does not necessarily conflict with Mary's journey to Bethlehem. As Thomas Hill has demonstrated, during ancient times and the Middle Ages "Syria" was a "generic term for the Holy Land" and denoted the geographical area that includes Israel and Judaea.[46] Bethlehem, in the kingdom of Judaea, therefore, would be embraced by the term "Syria." Moreover, Syria itself is mentioned by Luke in his description of Jesus's birth: he observes that the census which brought Mary to Bethlehem "took place while Quirinius was governor of Syria" (Luke 2:2–3). Furthermore, the phoenix's taking refuge in a "wēste stōwe" (169, "secret spot") of a "wudubearwe" (169, "woodland covert") harmonizes with the tradition that Mary was housed in a cave outside the city of Bethlehem.[47]

Birth

The investigation of the reflections of Mary and Mater Ecclesia in this Sequence centers on configurations that may be identifiable as the Tree of Jesse and the Apocalyptic woman clothed in the sun. The former is an especially powerful figure in that it unites the two major themes of the poem: life and death—in Christian terms, Incarnation and Passion—an association that is also to be found in the contemporary poem, *The Dream of the Rood* (90–94), where the Cross states that God honored it above all the trees in the wood, just as he honored his Mother above all women. Subsidiary images will also be examined in the light of a Christian view of the feminine dimension: they are the apple and the harvest.

The disobedience that came at the tree under which Adam and Eve ate the apple (400–405) is undone at a tree that may be thought of as the tree of obedience: it suggests simultaneously Christ's death on the tree of the Cross and Christ's birth—made possible by Mary's *fiat* to the angel's proposal—charted in the Tree of Jesse. That the tree in which the phoenix builds its nest is identified with the bird in name—"þone hātað men / fenix on foldan   of þæs fugles noman" (173–74, "The race of men / Call the tree of Phoenix   from the name of the fowl")—especially associates it with the Tree of Jesse, for this genealogical tree also takes its name from someone poised in it: Jesse, father of David and ancestor of Jesus; Jesse rests at the tree's base. Isaiah's prophecy of the Advent of Christ, "A shoot springs from the stock of Jesse, a scion thrusts from his roots" (Isaiah 11:1), gives rise to a complex iconographic and literary tradition in which the Incarnation and Passion are closely intertwined. The third-century African Father, Tertullian, is perhaps the first of the church fathers to interpret the shoot *(virgo)* as the Virgin Mary *(virgo)* and the blossom as Christ.[48] An instance in literature of the union of the Incarnation and Passion in the Tree of Jesse may be found in the eleventh-century homilies of Peter Damian. He follows his homily *In nativitate Beatissime Virginis Mariae* with one entitled, *De exaltatione Sanctae Crucis*, writing at the beginning of this last, *De virga Jesse deuenimus ad virgam crucis, et principium—redemptionis fine concludimus.*[49] ("From the shoot of Jesse we are brought to the blossom of the cross, and we conclude the beginning of redemption"). Medieval artists have also brought the Incarnation and Passion into relationship through the figure of the Tree of Jesse. An illumination in the Psalter and Hours of the Virgin, Morgan MS M. 729, fol. 345, combines the twelve branches of the Tree of Jesse with the two large branches forming the tree of the cross. Mary is implicated in both the life and the death of Christ by the sword drawn through her heart and the nest of birds placed above the head of the dead Christ. That the mother bird feeding her offspring is a figure of the pious pelican, a popular Christological picture type, is evident. The crescent moon shape of the bird's nest, however, as well as Mary's title, *Nidus Dei*,[50] may draw the Blessed Virgin into this figure. Even this small device seems to commingle the ideas of life and death. For while the nest is an obvious symbol of birth, the blood trickling over the nest reveals at what price th motheer feeds her young. Still another instance of the union in art of the Tree of Jesse and the Tree of the Cross is cited by Arthur Watson in his *Early Iconography of the Tree of Jesse.*[51] In the Cathedral of Sens, there is a sixteenth-century four-light window which not only combines the two trees but adds a slightly abbreviated inscription drawing on these familiar words of an early sixth-century hymn:

> Crux fidelis, inter omnes arbor una nobilis,
> Nullamtalem silua profert, flore, fronde, germine.
>
> [Faithful cross, noblest tree of all,
> The forest boasts no peer in blossom, leaf or shoot.]

When the phoenix, seeking seclusion, drives off its attendants and builds a nest in the high tree named for itself, we are brought to a kind of Tree of Jesse in which the two aspects of the drama of salvation, Incarnation and Passion, are viewed simultaneously. The same double vision

The Tree of Jesse combined with the Tree of the Cross. Morgan MS. M. 729, f. 345ᵛ. *(By permission of the Pierpont Morgan Library.)*

characterizes the peculiar nature of the phoenix's birth, intimately linked to death by the ashes out of which the new phoenix is formed. Appropriately, the same contrasting themes of life and death, Incarnation and Passion, function in a scriptural passage that the Old English poet may have had in mind as he recrafted the picture of the phoenix, pregnant in the light of the sun and anxious to give birth in the nest it prepares. That is the description of the woman clothed with the sun (Apocalypse 12:1–6) who gives birth to a child that is "taken straight up to God and to his throne." Apart from the overall resemblance of the general situations, a group of particular details create the association between the Old English and the scriptural passages. First there are the descriptions of weather. Before the woman clothed in the sun appears in Apocalypse 12:1, there has been a storm, "Then came flashes of lightning, peals of thunder and an earthquake, and violent hail (Apocalypse 11:19). The first word in Apocalypse 12:1, "Now," signals the shift to sunlight which comes with the appearance of the woman in labor. Likewise the phoenix, building its nest and drenched in the light of "heofones gim" (183, "heaven's bright gem"), the "wedercondel" (187, "weather candle"), comes on the scene only after a storm whose former presence is indicated by the adverb "Đonne" in the passage below:

> Đonne wind ligeð,　　　　weder bið fæger,
> ·　·　·　·　·　·　·　·　·　·
> bēoð wolcen tōwegen,　　　　wætra þrȳþe
> stille stondað,　　　biþ storma gehwylc
> āswefed under swegle, . . .
>
> 　　　　　　　　　　　　　　　　　　　　(182–86)

> [When the wind lies at rest　　　　and weather is fair,
> ·　·　·　·　·　·　·　·　·　·　·　·　·
> When clouds are dispersed　　　　and seas are tranquil
> And every storm　　　is still under heaven.]

Second, almost all theologians are in agreement that the woman of the Apocalypse may be viewed as a symbol of the Church of God of both the Old and New Covenants.[52] The heart of the phoenix as it constructs its nest is eager, we are told, to exchange its old age for youth (180–92). From the perspective of the phoenix as a symbol of Mary, her old age corresponds, naturally enough, to her life as a Jewess under the Old Covenant and her youth to the moment at the birth of Christ when she becomes the first Christian and archetype of the Church of the New Covenant. And further, it is generally recognized that the birth which takes place in Apocalypse 12 refers to more than merely Christ's birth in Bethlehem, for immediately after birth the child ascends to the throne of

God (12:5). Clearly, the birth referred to includes that rebirth of Christ experienced in the Resurrection after he arose from the dead. In the Christian view of the myth of the phoenix, the emergence of the new phoenix out of the ashes of the old has long been interpreted as the Resurrection of Christ as well as the general resurrection of all good Christians. Among the church fathers who have commented on the Christian significance of the phoenix, Tertullian, Zeno of Verona, Cyril of Jerusalem, and St. Ambrose, to name just a few, interpret the rebirth of the phoenix as a demonstration of the Resurrection.[53] As my examination of the images from the perspectives of primitive birth ritual and medieval embryology in chapter 4 indicates, it appears that in the treatment of the phoenix myth in the Latin and Old English poems there is also sufficient evidence of human, temporal birth to support the theme of Incarnation, certainly, at least, within the clearly Christian framework of the Old English poem. The numerous references to shelter, within the context of Christian allegory, may reflect the commonplace idea of Mary as the tabernacle of the Logos. As Calder rightly points out, the phoenix's building of its nest is an "act of creation."[54] The nest is described as a "hūs" (202, 212, 217, "house, home"), a "solere" (204, "lofty chamber") and a "willsele" (213, "hall"). It is, however, possible that at lines 212–13, where the sun is said to ignite the phoenix's house and fill the hall with steam, the words "hus" and "willsele" should be interpreted as referring not merely to the phoenix's nest but to its very body. Such an interpretation would, of course, make it even easier to see in these images of enclosed shelters reflections of the tabernacle image so commonplace in scriptural and patristic references to the Incarnation. To cite specific examples, we find the Johannine image of the Christ who "tabernacled" or "pitched his tent" among us when he became flesh (John 1:14) picked up in such representative passages on the Incarnation as these from Augustine and Rufinus respectively:

> Remaining in the bosom of His Father, He took possession of the womb of His Mother. In this bride-chamber, that is, in the womb of the Virgin, He united human to divine nature.[55]

> He who . . . was born ineffably from the Father had a shrine constructed for Him by the Holy Spirit in the recesses of the Virgin's womb.[56]

Viewed as either the phoenix itself or its nest, the "hūs" ignited by the sun is the most noble of God's creations. For its nobility, the phoenix merits a life in the earthly paradise where it enjoys all "londes frætwa" (150, "the world's beauty"), and when it builds its nest in the waste it draws on the best fruits of the earth, (194, "wyrta wynsume") and "wudublēda" (194, "fruits of the forest"). The theme of Christ's Incarnation within the noblest of humankind is understood by modern theologians to be an aspect of the woman of the Apocalypse. Eric May, for example, not only observes of the biblical woman that "she physically gave birth" but that if the iconography of "the sun, the moon, and the stars represent the glories of the Old and New Testament, then her [Mary's] singular privileges and virtues must be included."[57] One final detail that seems to associate the description of the phoenix's birth with that of the child in the Apocalypse is the eagle reference. In the Old English poem the newborn phoenix is said to look like an "earnes brid" (235, "eagle's young"). This reference to eagle parentage, not found in the Latin poem, suggests that the Old English poet could have had the scriptural passage in mind, for in Apocalypse 12:14 the mother of the child becomes eaglelike when she is "given a huge pair of eagle's wings to fly away from the serpent into the desert."

The homiletic second half of *The Phoenix* neither explicitly links the bird with Mary nor associates the nest with the Incarnation; nonetheless, both Mary and the Incarnation theme are implicit in the following verses about the construction of the nest in the high tree:

> Þǣr him nest wyrceð   wið niþa a gehwām
> dǣdum dōmlīcum   Dryhtnes cempa.
>
>   (451–52)

> [There God's warrior   weaves his nest,
> Safe from assault,   by virtuous deeds.]

These verses express the fulfillment of the Incarnation as it unfolds in the human life of the Church beyond Mary. The blessed Christian who is God's champion has accepted Mary's invitation to all members of her Church to allow the Word of God to fructify in themselves. How else is the Incarnation to be realized in the individual except through his good works? Through good works the individual exemplifies the obedient faith of Mary. Except to realize the effect of the Incarnation described in the actions of the "dryhtnes cempa" there would have been no need for him, who "hēah ofer heofonum   hālig wunade" (641, "high in heaven Holy abode"), to have a "cildes hād" (639," childhood") "on eorþan" (638, "on earth").[58]

One of the most imaginative ways in which the Old English poet has implicated the theme of Incarnation in the more obvious theme of Resurrection is through the image of the apple. The Anglo-Saxon poem is unique in its presentation of the phoenix's generation: the phoenix's development begins when out of ". . . þām āde   æples gelīcnes" (230, ". . . the ash of the pyre an apple's likeness") yields a "wyrm" (232, "worm"). About the significance of the ashes the homiletic commentary is clear: it is the death of which the life of Resurrection comes,

>   . . . fenix bēacnað
> geong in geardum   Godbearnes meaht
> þonne hē of ascan   eft onwæcned
> in līfes līf   leomum geþungen.

>   (646–49)

> [. . . the Phoenix fowl   with youth re-fashioned,
> When out of the ashes   he wakes again
> To the life of life   perfected in form,
> Is a symbol of the power   of the Son of God.]

The apple's role, however, in the regeneration of life is left for the reader to ponder. An obvious fruit that plays a role in Christian allegory is the apple that caused Eve to lose paradise; less obvious, perhaps, is another fruit that early church fathers delighted to compare to Eve's apple; that is, the fruit of the Virgin's womb. From the time of St. Irenaeus, born in Asia Minor and Bishop of Lyons in the second century, the drawing of antithetical parallels between Mary and Eve was a favorite way of indicating Mary's cooperation in the Redemption of the world.[59] By the time of St. Jerome (331–420) and his "Death by Eve, life by Mary," the Eve-Mary contrast had passed into proverb.[60] In a passage structured on typical Eve-Mary parallels, St. Thomas Aquinas includes the matter of contrasting fruits:

> Eve did not find what she wanted in her fruit; a sinner does not find what he wants in his sinfulness. This is why we seek out our fulfillment in the Fruit of the Virgin. And this Fruit is blessed by God for He has filled it with all graces.[61]

I would propose that the apple in the ashes from which the phoenix grows is Mary's fruit and, thus, provides the Anglo-Saxon poet with yet another means of intertwining the themes of Resurrection and Incarnation. The image of the apple merges, ten lines later, with another invention of the Old English poet: the evocation of a scene of harvest fruitfulness (243–57); just as the fruit of the old phoenix's (Mary's, subsequently, the Church's) womb develops into the new phoenix (Christ, subsequently, the good Christian), crops arise at harvest time out of the seeds sown in the earth. The image of the fields rich with "eorðan wæstmas" (243, "fruits of earth") functions as a figurative anticipation of the phoenix's return to the garden of the earthly paradise, prototype of Nature's plenitude. Indeed, the image of harvest fruitfulness suggests that the birth of the young phoenix has transformed the world into an imitation of the earthly paradise that earlier had only one solitary occupant, the Virgin in the garden.

The ease with which so many images inherited from primitive rites could be revalued for use within a Christian poem comes as no surprise. It was even obvious to Augustine, although he later disavowed the statement, that there were men practicing the Christian religion without knowing it from the beginning of the human race.[62] Although another African Father, Tertullian, seems not to include truly primitive peoples, he, too, citing the similarity between descriptions of the earthly paradise and the Elysian Fields of the classical poets, concludes that there must have been Christians before there was Christ incarnate (chapter 47 of his *Apology*). Perhaps that is why early poets and Fathers and Doctors of the Church have found the road between the phoenix and Christ and the phoenix and Mary-Ecclesia so easy to travel. Curiously, the road seems to lead to the same point: the start of things. Whereas the phoenix says of itself in the Egyptian hymn (in "Chapter of the coming forth by day out of the netherworld"), "I was yesterday," John writes of Christ that he "was with God in the beginning" (John 1:2) and Ecclesiasticus (24:9–20) speaks of Mary-Ecclesia as created "From eternity in the beginning."

6
EPILOGUE

Writing of the symbols in the rituals of the Ndembu tribe of Zambia, Victor Turner speaks of the symbol as the smallest "unit of specific structure in a ritual context."[1] In such a context, a symbol is part of an actual social action. Although a made thing like a poem is not fluid in the same way as a human activity, the poem, too, may be thought of as having symbols or images as its constituent elements. The first stanza of Charles Baudelaire's poem "Correspondances", which gives Turner the title for his book, suggests this idea both in its literal statement and in the images that join together to make the statement:

> La Nature est un temple où de vivants piliers
> Laissent parfois sortir de confuses paroles;
> L'homme y passe à travers de forêts de symboles
> Qui l'observent avec des regards familiers.[2]

> [Nature is a temple where the living pillars
> Emit from time to time confused words;
> There man passes through a forest of symbols
> Which observe him with familiar glances.]

These parallel signs of notation in ritual and literature have enabled me in the preceding chapters to explore the connotations of femininity in the symbols of Lactantius's *Carmen de Ave Phoenice* and the Old English *Phoenix* and the related symbols of female initiation ceremonies. The correspondences between the symbols of ritual and those in the poetic renderings of the myth of the phoenix bespeak similar visions of human existence in which the woman is the center of an endlessly repeated cycle of birth, death, and rebirth—itself a small pattern in a larger design. The phoenix myth has its genesis in ancient Egypt, an agrarian society that originally understood creation in terms of human reproduction. Also contained within the myth is the sense of cyclical time that Eliade and Ernest Cassirer identify as characteristic of early society wherein the rhythm of life followed more closely than ours the pattern of agriculture: each year it dies; each year life renews itself.[3] Because the female menstrual cycle is periodic and necessary to the perpetuation of a human cycle of life and death, it is easy to see why the myth of the phoenix proved a natural container for the central symbols and symbolic actions of female puberal rites. Like the myth, these rituals occur in societies that are predominantly agricultural and are, more often than not, organized on a matrilineal system, that is, the child's name and inheritance flow from the mother. How the phoenix myth, then, comes to be of service to an Anglo-Saxon poet whose tradition is markedly masculine—both with respect to the heroic poetry that typifies his age and as regards his chosen religion, Christianity, a patriarchal system—is at first puzzling. However, as I attempted to demonstrate in chapter 5, the Anglo-Saxon poet, in his translation and expansion of the Latin poem, takes advantage of the natural parallels between Resurrection and Incarnation, spiritual rebirth and natural birth, the Virgin Mary and Christ. The Marian dimension of *The Phoenix* suggests a wider and earlier manifestation of attention to the Virgin Mary than is generally claimed for her by scholars. There is, as I have shown, a growing awareness among students of art, philosophy, theology, and now literature of signs of Marian piety predating the twelfth century. Odilo, the tenth-century Abbot of Cluny, was not alone in his service to Mary, whom, because of her role as mother of God, author of creation, he addressed as "domina" and "regina."[4] In light of the fact that matriarchal religions are generally thought to view time as cyclical and self-renewing, it is of interest that Mary embodies the four characteristics which Carol Ochs isolates as typifying the major goddesses of all matriarchal religions: she is mother of God, bride of god, a virgin, and a mourner for her dead.[5] Indeed, it may be Mary, the feminine principle within Christianity, more than anything else, that has permitted the phoenix symbol to be adaptable to Christian needs.

The path that led to my reading of the phoenix poems does not stop at them. Pursued through later medieval literature, it passes many stations with familiar names where the potent, extensive presence of female symbolism has been half-noted, half-acknowledged or altogether unguessed. The impression left at the journey's end is that awe of the woman pervades the medieval imagination, forces hedonist and moralist to see the same reality, and draws the awed contemplator into the minutiae, the machinery, of that reality.

Water suggests many things, as do birds, gardens, trees, songs, and fire. But we have in front of us the results of an extensive thematic apperception test taken by the Medieval Poet, and the same association comes up again and again: it is woman—woman alluring, but more important, woman, the key to every vital operation in the observable world. Like Laudine in Chrétien's *Yvain*, she owns the fountain.

There is probably no place in medieval literature where the physical, fertile, blood-touched aspects of the woman are as intently the focus of the poet as in the phoenix poems. But if that can be granted, the later stations, the works where similar associations are made, are intensely engaging.

It would be ill advised at this point to linger over any of them, but it is hard to resist discussing a few, if only as a provocation to further research.

Yvain. If we recall the scene of the overflowing fountain in the Old English *Phoenix* and turn to that of the storm-making fountain in Chrétien de Troyes's twelfth-century romance, *Yvain*, we perceive a continuity of images—a tall tree by a spring; not a *single* bird but *many* birds perched on the branches of that tree; an open expanse of land—that sustains the sexual metaphor. The scene, however, appears not in a religious allegory like *The Phoenix* but in a courtly romance whose marvelous atmosphere Erich Auerbach has likened to that of the fairy tale.[6] The point of Auerbach's comparison is that, as in the case of fairy tales, the meaning of *Yvain*, and especially of its fountain adventure, can be penetrated only through the interpretation of symbols. The same could be said of dreams, and the account of Calogrenant's fountain adventure, told as it is outside the bedchamber of the sleeping king Arthur, is imbued with the spirit of an unconscious vision.

Calogrenant describes how, by following the direction of a herdsman, he created a storm at a fountain. At noon, when the sun—that generative power—approached its height, Calogrenant saw a basin hanging upon the tallest pine there ever was. From this obvious image of the erect phallus a basin of water is poured upon a stone containing four rubies that rests by the fountain:

> Plus flanboianz et plus vermauz,
> Que n'est au matin li solaus,
> Quant il apert an oriant.[7]

Why the red rubies beneath the perforations in the stone are made to remove the image of the receiving female organ from the core of the boiling spring, I do not know. But the ensuing storm above the spring, whose waters "boiloit come eve chaude" (432, "boiled like hot water" p. 185) is clearly a storm of sexual passion, the result of the conjunction of the male and female symbols. The birds, filling the tall pine with harmonious song immediately afterwards, may be seen as heralding the ecstatic calm after the storm of passion. The song of the singing birds is hardly savored before a knight, compared to an angry, warlike bird, comes on the scene; he is Esclados, husband of the lady whose fountain has been violated. The defender of the storm-making spring appears "plus tost qu'uns alerions" (487, "swifter than an eagle," p. 186), for the honor of his wife is at stake. That the spring symbolizes Laudine is evident not only from the imagery but from her own explicit reference to the spring as "ma fontainne" (2034, "My spring," p. 206). When it later becomes the knight Yvain's turn to present himself as a rival, both contending knights are described as birds: the mortally wounded husband flees as fast as "girfaus grue randone" (882, "a gerfalcon swoops upon a crane," p. 191), and Yvain, safely hidden in the husband's castle—as clear an analogue for his wife as the fountain—is a bird to ferret out like a partridge or quail (1267, p. 196).

The generative theme in the *Yvain* episode is expressed not merely in images that recall the phoenix poems but in symbols that evoke the sexual associations now familiar to us and the anthropological lore that prompted our first interest in the subject. Chrétien is, I think, developing a generative theme that grows out of the fountain episode; however, the theme takes on dimensions larger than the sexual elements operating in the scene, for the chapel placed beside the fountain signals another set of coordinates that must be taken into account.

Both Maxwell Luria and Tom Artin point to the liturgical red letter days of the romance: Pentecost and St. John the Baptist's Day (June 24th),[8] two feasts with obvious relationship to the sacrament of baptism.[9] The adventure of the fountain to which the herdsman points bears many resemblances to the sacrament that gives birth to Christian life. Perhaps most obvious is the chapel near the fountain, since from earliest Christian times the sites of churches were selected for their proximity to wells considered holy that might furnish water for use in baptism.[10] Also clear signs of the sacrament are the lightning bolts and various forms of water that descend on Calogrenant (and then Yvain):

> Mes trop an i versai, ce dot;
> Que lors vi le ciel si derot,
> Que de plus de quatorze pars
> Me feroit es isuz li esparz,
> Et les nues tot pesle mesle
> Gitoient noif et pluie et gresle.[11]

(439–44)

They are the water of penance and the fire of grace. Less evident, however, is the significance of the two conflicts with Esclados, the different outcomes of which distinguish Calogrenant's failure from Yvain's success. Success takes Yvain to Laudine's castle (on the edge of the true paradise) and failure brings Calogrenant back to the castle of the vavasour (near a false paradise). After the storm is raised, Esclados comes looking not only like a swift eagle but ". . . come mautalantis /

Vint . . . Fiers par sanblant come lions" (486–88, "as if with evil intent, came . . . looking as fierce as a lion," p. 186). In scripture the lion has a double symbolism. It may, as in the case of the lion in the second half of *Yvain*, signify Christ as the Lion of Judah (Revelation 5:5) or, as in this instance, it may represent the evil spirit who "goeth about as a roaring lion seeking whom he may devour" (1 Peter 5:8). That the metaphor identifies Esclados as demonic is suggested by the traditional symbolism of lions so frequently placed below baptismal fonts to depict visually the subjugation of evil by the power of the waters of baptism.[12] The struggle with Esclados recalls the confrontation between the catechumen and Satan through which man participates in Christ's Passion, specifically the Harrowing of Hell, the key event in the drama of redeeming humanity from enslavement to the devil.

In the struggle with Esclados, Calogrenant fails where Yvain succeeds, but he is, nevertheless, granted the grace of baptism. Like Yvain, he is permitted the sight and sound of the birds in the pine tree who ". . . chantoient / Si que mout bien s'antracordoient. / Mes divers chanz chantoit chascuns" (465–67, "sang in harmony, yet the note of each was different," p. 186). Calogrenant has undoubtedly heard with an understanding heart (Cf. 151–52, p. 182). If as he says, "Les oroilles sont voie et doiz, / Par ou s'an vient au cuer la voiz" (165–66, "The ears are the path and channel by which the voice can reach the heart," p. 182), there is no doubt that he has listened intelligently, for the sound fills him with joy, bliss, and rapture. Luria suggests that the birds are probably those usually pictured in iconographic representations of the *fons vitae*.[13]

Laudine, who speaks of the fountain as her own ("ma fontainne," 2034), and Lunete, her messenger-representative who helps keep the fountain defended, underscore the maternal aspects of the fountain and the generative powers of the waters of baptism. Each woman is closely associated with the fountain. Yvain links the fountain with Laudine as clearly as she does herself; the mere sight of it causes such a sense of her loss that the exiled Yvain considers suicide:

> "Que faz je, las? que ne m'oci?
> Comant puis je demorer ci
> Et veoir les choses ma dame?"[14]

(3533–35)

And at the end of the tale, when Lunete goes to find Yvain for the purposes of bringing him back to Laudine, it is by the fountain that she finds him (6659ff.). Probably Lunete's most definite physical tie to the fountain occurs in the second half of the romance when she is imprisoned in the chapel next to it. The effect of these physical links

Baptismal font of Saint Mary's Church, Stafford, England. *(Courtesy of Peter Rogers.)*

The *fons vitae*. Paris, Bibliothèque Nationale, MS. lat. 1203 fol. 3vo. *(By permission of the Bibliothèque Nationale.)*

between the two women and the fountain merge them with its symbolism and in turn imbue the fountain with their womanly qualities of nurturing protectiveness, the dominant aspect of the female nature that each shows Yvain. Lunete hides him from would-be murderers, out to avenge the death of Esclados, and feeds him (907–1054), and Laudine also shields him from physical harm when she gives him a magic ring (2600–2608).

It may be more accurate to say that the female characters do not so much lend a maternal coloration to the fountain symbolism as emphasize the female dimension already implicit in it as a baptismal image, for from earliest Christian times the water of baptism has been commonly thought of as giving birth to a new creature. Holy Mother Church's well of grace, or *fons vitae*, permits the Christian knight to evade death, when his cycle of earthly life is complete, by entering the world of eternity.

Floire et Blancheflor. Another twelfth-century French romance, *Floire et Blancheflor,* presents several symbols and ideas that are analogous to those already encountered in *The Phoenix.* First there is the matter of a repeated cycle of life and death—this one involving a series of women rather than phoenixes and a period of one year rather than a thousand.

A certain emir of Babylon—one of those ancient cities that, like Egypt, saw in the human cycle of birth and death a reflection of the parallel cycle in Nature—established the practice of killing his wife at the end of every year and replacing her with another. If one thinks of the wives as a class rather than as hapless individuals, the new wife is as effectively reborn as the new phoenix of the myth. Indeed, like the old phoenix, the old wife dies in flames. Her death by fire is directly linked to her inability to pass a chastity test that takes place annually over a spring in the middle of the emir's walled garden on the Euphrates:

> Quant li amirals veut sortir,
> Ses puceles il fait venir
> Au ruissel de la fontanele,
> Dont de fin or est la gravele.
> Quant passer doivent le canal,
> Qui est d'argent et de cristal.
> Outre en-vont ordenéement;
> Et il au passer moult entent,
> Et a sa gent i fait entendre.
> Grant merveille i puet on aprendre
> Car, quant il i passe puoele,
> Lors est li eve clere et bele,
> Et au passer de feme cue,
> L'ove on est eués toute móue.

Cele qui par cou est provee
Desfaite est et fu jetee.[15]

(1801–16)

[When the time comes for the emir
To choose, he summons his girls here
To the fresh spring waters which travel
Rippling o'er emeralds and gravel.
When the maids come to cross the flume
Which crystal and silver illume,
They make the crossing one by one,
While he pays close attention
To them, and so too do his kings.
Now you shall hear astounding things:
When a virgin crosses, the rill
Remains transparent, pure and still
While one whom man has known will spoil
Its calm, will muddy it and roil.
Such a one's end is grim and dire.
She's slain and cast into a fire.][16]

The spring that reacts to the sexually active woman by becoming muddy reflects an apparently innate sense of pollution or of the turbulence of sexual passion.[17] One wonders if the phoenix's menstrual fountain lurks behind this diviner of passion and pollution—especially since the garden setting for this activity is drenched in vermilion. Above the spring grows a tree:

Por cou que tous tans i a flors,
On l'apele l'arbre d'amors:
L'une renaist quant l'autre chiet.
Par grant maistrise l'arbre siet:
L'arbre, la flor, tout est vermeus.
De fisique et cil bons conseus
Qui l'planta: car l'asséoir
Fu fais l'engiens si com j'espoir.
Au main, quant lieve li soleus,
En l'arbre fiert tres-tous vermeus,
Et avoec li fierent doi vent,
Par qu'est tenus tempréement.

(1787–98)

[The Tree of Love, men call
It. 'Tis in bloom perpetual:
As each flower falls, one comes to fill
Its place. The tree was placed with skill.
Vermilion are both tree and flowers.

He was endowed with magic powers
Who planted it. For such sagacity
Guided the placing of the tree,
The orient-rising morning sun
Pours its vermilion rays upon
It, while two winds that blow and meet
There serve to moderate the heat.]

(p. 75)

Tree, flower, sun—all are vermilion, like the phoenix (and the four rubies by Yvain's storm-making fountain). And, too, as each vermilion flower falls, another takes its place—an eternal cycle like that of the phoenix and that in which the emir's wives are caught up. One last point of resemblance: the emir's garden resounds with the song of birds.

Romance of the Rose. The quest for the Rose in the thirteenth-century *Romance of the Rose* is as much a sexual metaphor as the quest for the storm-making fountain in *Yvain.* Whereas Yvain encounters the woman, source of generation, first symbolically in the fountain and then actually in its various incarnations—Lunete, Laudine, and, perhaps, the woman healer of the forest—the Lover of the *Romance,* also discovering the woman through the symbol of the fountain, never encounters her as a character more defined than the Rose.

The Lover's discovery of the Rose occurs in a scene by the fountain that brings together the, by now, familiar configuration of tree, well, and bird. In Guillaume's description of the well of Narcissus under the shadow of the pine in the Garden of Diversion the bird is not present except as a metaphoric detail:

Car Cupido, li filz Venus
Sema d'amors ici la graine,
Qui toute acuere la fontaine,
E fist ses laz enuiren tendre,
E ses angins i mist, por prendre
Demoiseillis e demoisiaus;
Qu' Amors si ne uelt autre oisiaus.
Por la graine qui fu semée
Fu ceste fontaine apelée.
La Fontaine d'Amors par droit.[18]

(1588–97)

[For it is here that Cupid, son of Venus, sowed the
seed of love that has dyed the whole fountain, here
that he stretched his nets and placed his snares to
trap young men and women; for Love wants no other
birds. Because of the seed that was sown this fountain
has been rightly called the Fountain of Love.][19]

However, this metaphor is an integral part of the transformation of the well image into a bird trap that catches the only "birds" such a trap can catch: "men and women." The trapper, Cupid, the winged God of Love, enhances the bird character of the well, for he is earlier described as completely covered with birds: parrots, nightingales, calendar-larks, and tit-mice (900–06). Moreover, the siren-sound of birds singing is what tempts the Lover to find the entrance to the garden with the well at its center in the first place (497). In a literal sense, the garden is the Beloved's private parts.

In his study of the iconography of *The Romance of the Rose*, John Fleming notes that the well which brought death to Narcissus and ensnared the Lover, as well, appears in one of the manuscript illustrations as a poisoned well marked with the appropriate designation for poison, a death's head.[20] In view of the obvious womblike associations of the well in which the Lover catches his first glimpse of the Rose reflected in the magic crystals, one wonders if there might be some lingering hint of the menses about the dye in the well, for the poisonous effects on men of the catamenia have a long and well-explored history.[21] The suggestion of the catamenia, if plausible at all, would offer only the most literal explanation of the perilous well. At a deeper fold of meaning, what poisons the well, of course, is love sought as an end itself; unproductive love generates death, not life. Narcissus scorns Echo to love a sterile image of himself, and the Lover who stares into the well is likewise guilty of self-love.

For a rose worthy to be loved the Lover should look to the celestial Rose of the garden in Jean de Meun's continuation of the *Romance*. There in the Park of the Good Shepherd, antithesis of the Garden of Diversion, it grows where the Lover finds, instead of the perilous well,

> . . . la fontaine de vie
> Par desouz l'olive foillie
> Qui porti le fruit de salu.
>
> (20521–23)

> [. . . the fountain of life
> beneath the leafy olive tree that
> bears the fruit of salvation.]
>
> (p. 336)

But the Lover prefers loving *par amour* to salvation. Presumably, if the Lover were prepared to love fruitfully, natural love might be made to lead to God. Jean de Meun's Genius, Priest of Nature, teaches that those who love each other loyally are saved by God from Death (19529–37), and Nature has earlier made clear that loyal love is the kind that leads to

procreation. Nature enunciates a doctrine of plenitude wherein the prototype that one passes on to offspring in order to sustain the species is
envisioned as the eternal phoenix within the individual. Nature's explanation of the importance of procreation is based on this analogy to the
phoenix:

> C'est fenis la comune fourme
> Que Nature es pieces refourme,
> Qui dou tout perdue serait,
> Qui l'autre vivre ne lairait.
> Cete maniere neis ont
> Trestoutes les choses qui sont
> Desouz le cerole de la lune.

(15995–16001)

> [It is the phoenix in its ideal common form that
> Nature reshapes into individuals; and this common
> form would be entirely lost if the next phoenix were
> not left alive. All things under the circle of the moon
> have this very same mode of being.]

(p. 271)

The question is, then, is the Lover a dead bird, so to speak, by the end of
the poem? I think not. He awakes from the dream as soon as he plucks
the red rose and he, like Calogrenant—and Dante—lives to tell his story.
The love quest, five years afterwards, appears to have transformed itself
into a quest with a celestial end. If we regard the *Romance* as a unified
work, Guillaume's first half is where we begin the account: the month is
May; the time lapse, five years; the dreamer, alive to tell his story. Both
the month and the number five suggest his dedication is now to a
particular Rose—the Virgin Mary: "C'est cele qui tant a de pris / E tant est
dine d'estre amee / Qu'el doit estre Rose clamee" (41–44, "She who is so
precious and so worthy to be loved that she should be called Rose," p.
31). The young Lover is a phoenix, after all, who wins the second
chance.

The *Vox Clamantis* (c. 1386) of "moral Gower" offers a curious instance
of weaving phoenix and Marian references—positive touchstones for the
moralizing Jean de Meun—into a description of "a comely woman, for
lust of whom knights' hearts are ensnared and very often left destitute of
rational judgement."[22] Gower catalogs every lovely, dangerous part;
borrows inappropriately from Peter Riga's *Aurora* a description of the
Virgin Mary: "The girl's beauty transcends humankind; she possesses a
kind of divinity which surpasses the race of man"; then finishes the
portrait with what seems almost an afterthought: "she becomes a phoe-

nix without peer."[23] Accidental as the climactic reference appears to be, Gower could not have chosen a more potent image for the power—even *dangerous* power—of woman.

Parlement of Foules. Of the numerous critics who have studied Chaucer's *Parlement*, perhaps Dorothy Bethurum isolated most succinctly the basic issue of the poem: "Whatever other facets this poem may have, it is essentially a love poem, and it is about fertility and generation."[24] Her purpose in writing her article was to correct what she viewed as a failure of *Parlement* criticism up to her time: its neglect of the Garden of Love. That landscape contains so much which is relevant to our purpose—the Temple of Venus, the place "so sote and grene" (295)[25] of the Goddess Nature, the huge assembly of birds—that we will not hesitate to explore what in the garden there is that recalls symbols and ideas we have seen at work in the phoenix poems.

As much from the popular conception of the bird as a favorite baby-bringing symbol as from my treatment of the phoenix poems in terms of the generative cycle of the female, the bird is recognizable as a conventional symbol of fertility. Just as in the development of the myth of the phoenix the fabulous bird has appeared in relationship to female goddesses, pagan and Christian—Isis, Venus, the Virgin Mary—the birds who assemble on Valentine's Day to choose their mates are brought within the sphere of a goddess, "this noble Goddess Nature" (303). The entire *amorosa visione* containing Nature, in fact, appears to have been the result of the inspiration of a goddess, the goddess of Love,

> Cytherea! thow blysful lady swete,
> That with thy fyrbrond dauntest whom the lest,
> . . . madest me this sweven for to mete.
>
> (113–15)

J. A. W. Bennett observes of the figure of Nature that "as Bernardus Silvestris (who first gives Nature life in medieval allegory) has described her by a phrase echoing the Salutation to the Virgin: *Natura uteri mei beata fecundatus:* so Chaucer applies to her a phrase from the same Salutation: 'full of grace.' "[26] It is as if a primary allegorical dimension of the Anglo-Saxon phoenix had been isolated and incorporated into a separate entity who is rechristened "Nature!" Chaucer's goddess oversees the pairing of her bird subjects by which the continuity of society proceeds:

> Ne there nas foul that cometh of engendrure
> That they no were prest in here presence,
> To take hire dom and yeve hire audyence
>
> (306–8)

Although the birds, like humans, complicate the process of selection with a debate on, among other matters, fidelity in marriage, the purpose of the parliament remains one: the choice of marriage partners.

It is probably fair to say, without being reductive, that Bethurum's emphasis on the garden as the center of the poem "giving design to all the rest" leads attention to the crux of Chaucer's difficult juxtapositions.[27] Chaucer superimposed a garden of steamy lust on one representative of productive love without creating easy reconciliations—unlike the two gardens of the *Romance of the Rose*, both garden areas, the Temple of Venus and the flowery hill of Nature, are within a single enclosure.

After receiving Africanus's assurance that neither the invitation inscribed on the gateway to the garden of love nor the warning—"th'eschewing is the only remedye!"—applies to him, the dreamer is shoved into the precincts of the garden. When the dreamer sees the garden within the gate, his response is immediately joyous: "But, Lord, so I was glad and wel begoon!" (171). As he goes on to describe the scene, it is unclear whether the source of his joy is a simple *locus amoenus* of secular delights or the allegorical scenic elements that denote paradise, so many images are shared in common: trees perpetually green, a garden by a river, a green meadow, many-colored flowers, angelic-voiced birds singing in branches of trees.

Just as it begins to appear that the dreamer has followed the happy road described on the gate's invitation, he comes upon a scene of unrest that has no place in paradise. There by a well under a tree is "Cupid, oure lorde" (212). His well attracts a crowd of figures (i.e., Lust, Craft, Flattery, Foolhardynesse) who remind us of the gate's warning that "likerous folk" (78–79) would be punished. As if this throng were not enough to make clear that this is not the "welle of grace" described in the gate's invitation, Chaucer adds further that Cupid's arrows are hardened in the well, "Some for to sle, and some to wound and kerve" (217). The well is thus a well of pain, not grace, having some relationship surely to the "sorweful were" described in the gate's warning inscription. The following description of Venus's temple, peopled with sated, jealous lovers and decorated with stories about those who died for love, ratifies the suspicion that the dreamer may be in the part of the garden to be eschewed. The Temple of Venus in the midst of paradise proves that the scene of innocence is only apparent and the gates enclose a world much like our own, offering delights both heavenly and earthly. The dreamer does, in fact, at the end of the Cupid and Venus passage, find himself back in the paradisial section of the park where the benevolent figure of creative Nature, "vicaire of the almyghty Lord" (379), presides over the parliament of birds eager for mating. As orchestrator of the forces of fecundity, Nature is surely an agent of the gate's invitation to the "welle of grace."

If there is a lesson to be deduced from Chaucer's juxtapositions of the hill of Nature and the Temple of Venus, can it be related profitably to the phoenix? Donald Baker's view of the contrasts is serviceable—"Love is good, although the abuse of love is reprehensible"[28]—but susceptible to a dangerous misinterpretation; that is, that Chaucer's "lesson" is that natural love, unchecked, might become a substitute for love of God. Such a view would turn Chaucer's warm humanity cold. Chaucer's poem does not say we must get beyond earthly love; no, rather we need to find our way to it—"The lyf so short, the craft so long to lerne." The way to draw closer to God is to enter the gateway and approach the fountain of love, even at the price of pain. For Chaucer, as for Chrétien, the "welle of grace" shares space with the "sorweful were."

The real lesson of Chaucer's *Parlement* is the lesson of the phoenix at the fountain. When natural love becomes a mode of charity, it is creative and partakes of the divine energy out of which, in the beginning, God created lovable creatures out of Love. It moves man from the form of the fountain to the Fountain, from "the phoenix in its ideal common form" (to borrow Jean de Meun's words) to the phoenix itself.

This is a long way to come from the first insight into the vision behind the phoenix, but it is by no means the last discovery that will be drawn from the myth of the cyclic bird and its well. So elemental are the experiences of female fertility that one could almost have predicted, as astronomers predict yet unsighted stars, the treatment of the two in literature. The star has been found. What glimmerings there were in sexual and spiritual interpretations of this or that water source in medieval literature are heightened by the discovery of the big symbolic statement behind the phoenix, and the interpreter can be emboldened in the future to test bird, tree, water, song, and all the other surveyed symbols to see if they do not bespeak an even blunter reference than hitherto conceded to our intertwined sexual and eternal natures.

NOTES

Many of the works cited below are contained in the following collections:

Corpus Scriptorum Ecclesiasticorum Latinorum (Vienna: C. Geroldi & Sons, 1866–1913).

Jean Hubaux and Maxime Leroy, *Le Mythe du Phénix dans les Littératures, Grecque et Latine* (Liège: Faculté de philosophie et lettres; Paris: E. Droz, 1939).

Jacques Paul Migne, *Patrologiae cursus completus* (Paris: J. P. Migne, 1844 onwards).

I frequently refer to the *Patrologia Latina* and *Patrologia Graeca* of Migne by volume and column numbers. Citations to *Le Mythe du Phénix* appear as Hubaux and Leroy.

Prologue

1. See my "Wells and Streams in Three Chaucerian Gardens," *Papers on Language & Literature* 15 (1979): 339–56 and "A Reconsideration of the Wine Cask Figure in the *Reeve's Prologue,*" *Chaucer Review* 15(1980): 37–43.

2. For what little biographical information there is about Lactantius consult Berthold Altaner, *Patrologie* (Freiburg: Herder & Co., 1950), 153–54; the introduction to *Lactantius' Epitome of the Divine Institutes,* ed. and trans. E. H. Blakeney (London: S.P.C.K., 1950), ix; N. F. Blake, ed. the introduction to *The Phoenix* (Manchester: Manchester University Press, 1964), 18; and *Encyclopedia Britannica,* 11th ed., s.v. *Lactantius Firmianus.*

3. T. O. Ranger and I. N. Kimambo, eds. Introduction to *The Historical Study of African Religion* (London: Heinemann, 1972), 2.

4. J. H. Breasted, *Ancient Records of Egypt* (Chicago: University of Chicago, 1906), 1:333–36 and 353.

5. Basil Davidson, *The African Past* (London: Longmans, 1964), 11. As more early-Iron Age material is discovered in East Africa and adjacent territories and as more radio carbon dates become available, some questions have been raised about the original lines of diffusion. There are many who have argued for routes of diffusion from Meroe in the Middle Nile to Lake Chad, among them S. M. Cole in *The Prehistory of East Africa,* 2nd ed. (London: Macmillan, 1963), 301; B. M. Fagan in *Southern Africa during the Iron Age* (New York: F. A. Praeger, 1965), 48–49; and Merrick Posnansky in *Prelude to East African History* (London: Oxford University Press, 1966), 87–90. But J. G. G. Sutton may be right when he says, "The final picture will doubtless be more complex: it will not be a question of whether iron first arrived in East Africa from Meroe or the Zambezi, from West Africa, Ethiopia or the Indian Ocean, but of recognizing a combination of broad fronts" ("The Interior of East Africa" in *The African Iron Age,* ed. P. L. Shinnie, [Oxford: Clarendon Press, 1971], 142).

6. Davidson, *African Past*, 11.

7. Wilfred H. Schoff, trans. *The Periplus of the Erythraean Sea* (New York: Longmans, Green, & Co., 1912), 28.

8. H. N. Chittick, "The Coast of East Africa," in Shinnie, *African Iron Age*, 109.

9. Ibid., 118.

10. Ibid., 118, 113.

11. From *Primitive Culture* (1871), a selection of which is reprinted in Richard Dorson, *The British Folklorists: A History* (London: Routledge and Kegan Paul, 1968), 193ff.

12. Jeff Opland, *Anglo-Saxon Oral Poetry: A Study of the Traditions* (New Haven and London: Yale University Press, 1980), 12.

13. Ranger and Kimambo, 11.

14. Cleanth Brooks, "Implications of an Organic Theory of Poetry," in *Literature and Belief, English Institute Essays (1957)*, ed. Meyer H. Abrams (New York: Columbia University Press, 1958), 72.

Chapter 1. Introduction

1. Renewal follows upon decay in *The Letter of St. Clement of Rome to the Corinthians*, trans. Frances X. Glimm, S. T. L. (New York: CIMA Publishing, 1947), ch. 25–26; Tacitus's *Annals*, trans. John Jackson (London: William Heinemann, 1931), 6. 28; and Ambrose's *De excessu Fratris* 2. 59 (*Patrologia Latina* 15, col. 1331) and *Hexameron* 5. 23, 79 (*Patrologia Latina* 14, col. 238).

2. Renewal follows burning in the *Physiologus*, the *Apocalypse* of the Pseudo-Baruch, ch. 6–8, Lactantius's *Carmen de Ave Phoenice*, Claudian's *Phoenix*, and the Old English *Phoenix*. The main edition of the Old English poem is N. F. Blake's. Reliable texts of the other works may be found in the original with parallel French translations in Hubaux and Leroy, xi–xxxvi. Both traditions of renewal appear in different contexts in Pliny's *Natural History*, trans. W. H. S. Jones (London: William Heinemann, 1951), 10. 4 and 24. 29.

3. R. van den Broek, *The Myth of the Phoenix* (Leiden: E. J. Brill, 1972), 106.

4. Robert Graves, *The White Goddess* (New York: Creative Age Press, 1948), 34.

5. R. T. Rundle-Clark, "The Origin of The Phoenix," *University of Birmingham Historical Journal* 2(1949–50): 112.

6. Ibid.

7. The Egyptian hieroglyph for "well full of water": ᴡᴡ is also used to mean "vulva." See Sir Alan Gardiner, *Egyptian Grammar*, 3rd ed. (London: Oxford University Press, 1957), 492.

8. Information furnished by Dr. Klaus Helfrich, Museum für Völkerkunde; Berlin, Germany.

9. Hermann H. Ploss and Max Bartels, *Woman: An Historical, Gynaecological, and Anthropological Compendium*, ed. Eric Dingwall (London: William Heinemann, 1935), 1:651.

10. M. Esther Harding, *Woman's Mysteries: Ancient and Modern* (New York: Harper Colophon Books, 1971), 51.

11. It may be worth observing that the moon's cycle of waxing and waning is parallel to the phoenix's cycle of dying and resurrection—a pattern usually compared to the sun's cycle of rising and setting.

12. Anita Spring, "Women's Rituals and Natality Among the Luvale of Zambia," (Ph.D. diss., Cornell University, 1976), 135.

13. Hubaux and Leroy, xxxv.

14. Van den Broek, *Myth of the Phoenix*, 296.

15. Clement of Alexandria, *The Miscellanies* 5. 7 ("The Egyptian Symbols and Enigmas of Sacred Things"), in *Writings*, trans. William Wilson (Edinburgh: Clark, 1868–9), 2:246.

16. Marija Gimbutas, *The Gods and Goddesses of Old Europe 7,000 to 3,500 B.C.: Myths, Legends, and Cult Images* (Berkeley: University of California, 1974), 106–7.

17. Ibid., 102.

18. Rundle-Clark, "Origin of the Phoenix," 4.

19. Gimbutas, *Gods and Goddesses of Old Europe*, 135.

20. Mircea Eliade, *Myths, Dreams and Mysteries*, trans. Philip Mairet (New York: Harper Torchbooks, 1960), 175.

21. Gimbutas, *Gods and Goddesses of Old Europe*, 143.

22. Ibid., 149.

23. Harding, *Women's Mysteries*, 52.

24. Sir James C. Frazer, "The Magic Art and the Evolution of Kings," *The Golden Bough*, Part 1 (New York: Macmillan & Co. 1917), 1:36–37.

25. Harding, *Woman's Mysteries*, 116.

26. In connection with the Menstrual Sequence, a speculation of Alexander Marshack is noteworthy (*The Roots of Civilization: The Beginnings of Man's First Art, Symbol and Notation* [New York: McGraw-Hill, 1972]). A group of Upper Paleolithic feminine images that tend to be joined to animals, among them birds, seem to Marshack to have menstrual significance—particularly those ochered red—and to form a continuous tradition of representation with later Neolithic figurines such as the Bird Goddesses analyzed by Gimbutas. He regards the Upper Paleolithic feminine images as "part of the intellectual, time-factored and time-factoring heritage that prepared the way for agriculture" (305), and their area of dispersion is vast: Europe, Asia, Africa, and the Americas (336).

27. Eliade, *Myths, Dreams, and Mysteries*, 217.

28. Ibid, 197.

29. Mircea Eliade, *Rites and Symbols of Initiation*, trans. Willard R. Trask (New York: Harper Torchbooks, 1965), 60.

30. Ibid., 126.

31. C. S. Lewis, "The Anthropological Approach," in *English and Medieval Studies Presented to J. R. R. Tolkien on the Occasion of his 70th Birthday*, ed. Norman Davis and C. L. Wrenn (London: G. Allen & Unwin, 1962), 221.

32. Flavius Sosipater Charisius, *Artis Grammaticea* 5, ed. Carl Barwick (Leipzig: B. G. Teubner, 1925), 376. Translations into English are mine unless otherwise indicated. Wherever possible I have tried to cite authoritative translations.

33. Willy Morel, ed., *Fragmenta Poetarum Latinorum Epicorum et Lyricorum Praeter Ennium et Lucilium* (Leipzig: B. G. Teubner, 1927), 60.

34. See text in Hubaux and Leroy, xxvii (Greek) and xxix (French translation).

35. H. de la Ville de Mirmont, *Études sur l'Ancienne Poesie Latine* (Paris: A. Fontemoing, 1903), 301.

36. In Latin the phoenix is of feminine gender and is translated "she" in Mary Cletus Fitzpatrick's edition and translation of *Lactanti De Ave Phoenice* (Ph. D.diss., University of Pennsylvania, 1933). (Her Latin text and translation are referred to throughout my study.) In Old English, however, the phoenix is masculine. See chap. 5 for discussion of this point.

37. Hubaux and Leroy, 5.

38. Claudian's text is printed in Hubaux and Leroy, xxi–xxiii; xxi, 17–20.

39. Dracontius, "Romulea," in *Fl. Merobaodis Reliqviae Blossii Aemilu Dracontii*

Carmina Evgenii Toletani Episcopi Carmina Et Epistvlae, ed. Fridericvs Vollmer (Berlin: Apvd. Weidmanos, 1905), 183.

40. Tacitus, *Annals* 6.28.

41. Van den Broek, *Myth of the Phoenix,* 26.

42. Ibid., 27.

43. *Encyclopedia Britannica,* 11th ed., s.v. *Egypt.*

44. Hubaux and Leroy, 26.

45. Wilhelm Roscher, *Lexikon* (Leipzig: B. G. Teubner, 1924–37), 2, col. 434, 1. 21, s.v. *Isis.*

46. Beryl Rowland, *Birds with Human Souls* (Knoxville: University of Tennessee, 1978), 84.

47. George R. S. Mead, *Thrice-Greatest Hermes* (London: The Theosophical Society, 1906), 1:333.

48. Harding, *Woman's Mysteries,* 185. Of tangential interest, in the light of the phoenix-crocodile-Venus-Isis connections made in this chapter, is an examination by Alice Miskimin of the Isis church episode in Spenser's *Faerie Queene* called "Britomart's Crocodile and the Legends of Chastity," *Journal of English and Germanic Philology* 77 (1978): 17–36.

49. Harding, *Woman's Mysteries,* 185.

50. Ibid., 190

51. Quoted (and translated) by Van den Broek, *Myth of the Phoenix,* 35. This portion of the Utrecht fragment is to be found in Kopt. Ms. no. K. 9666-7 of the collection of Archduke Rainer, now in the Austrian National Library, Vienna.

52. Translated by Van den Broek, *Myth of the Phoenix,* 47.

53. In Rufinus Tyrannius especially, the phoenix is said to represent the virginity of Mary and the incarnation of Christ (*Commentarius in Symbol.* 11, *Patrologia Latina* 21, col. 350): "Omnis partus ex tribus (ut opinor) constat: si adultae aetatis sit femina, si virum adeat, si non sit illius vulva vitio sterilitatis occulsa. Ex his tribus in hoc partu, quem praedicamus, unum defuit, vir scilicet: et hanc partem (quia qui nascebatur non erat terrenus homo, sed caelestis) per spiritum caelestem dicimus, salva Virginis incorruptione, completam. Et tamen quid mirum videtur, si virgo conceperit, cum Orientis avem, quam Phoenicem vocant, in tantum sine conjuge nasci, vel renasci constet, ut semper una sit, et semper sibi ipsi nascendo, vel renascendo succedat?" [All births (according to common opinion), derive from three things: the woman's being of adult age, the entrance of the man, and the freedom from sterility of the woman's vulva. One of these three was missing from the birth that we are now discussing, namely the man, and we say that this birth (since the one born of it was not an earthly man but a heavenly one) was effected through the heavenly spirit and left the virgin intact. But what is remarkable about the conception by a virgin when that eastern bird which they call the Phoenix is likewise born without a spouse—or rather reborn so that it always remains one and always succeeds itself by being born or reborn?] See also Commodian, *Carmen Apologeticum* 139–40 (*Patrologia Latina* 5, col. 260) Epiphanius, *Ancoratus* 84 (*Patrologia Greca* 43, col. 174), Pseudo-Epiphanius, *Physiologus* 11 (*Patrologia Greca* 43, col. 526–27), Petrus Damascenus 52.11 (*Patrologia Latina* 145, col. 773).

Chapter 2. The Menstrual Sequence

1. Two of the most notable works that articulate this view are Graves's *White Goddess* and Mario Praz's *The Romantic Agony* (London: Oxford University Press, 1933).

2. O. F. Raum, "Female Initiation Among the Chaga," *American Anthropologist*, n.s., 41(1939): 559.

3. Audrey Richards, *Chisungu: A Girl's Initiation Ceremony Among the Bemba of Northern Rhodesia* (London: Faber & Faber, 1956), 121.

4. Phyllis M. Kaberry, *Aboriginal Woman, Sacred and Profane* (London: George Routledge & Sons, 1939), 235.

5. Ibid.

6. Bruno Bettelheim, *Symbolic Wounds* (New York: Collier Books, 1962), 97.

7. Kaberry, *Aboriginal Woman*, 235.

8. Horapollo, *The Hieroglyphus of Horapollo Nilous*, trans. Alexander T. Cory (London: W. Pickering, 1840), 2:57.

9. Alfred Wiedemann, *Religion of the Ancient Egyptians* (New York: G. P. Putnam, 1897), 162.

10. Ibid., 167.

11. Ibid., 163.

12. See chap. 1.

13. Ibid.

14. Van den Broek, *Myth of the Phoenix*, 296ff.

15. A. C. Haddon, *Decorative Art of British New Guinea* (Dublin: Royal Irish Academy, 1894), 196–99, 209–10 and figures 184–205.

16. Richards, *Chisungu*, 82.

17. Ibid., 59.

18. Ibid., 84.

19. Ibid., 175.

20. H. Cory, *African Figurines: Their Ceremonial Use in Puberty Rites in Tankanyika* (London: Faber and Faber, 1956), 26.

21. Ibid., 41.

22. Ibid., 154.

23. See chap. 1.

24. Citations to Lactantius's *Carmen* may be found in Fitzpatrick's edition (cited earlier). The English translations are also hers and appear in her text opposite the Latin verse.

25. Throughout the study I cite N. F. Blake's edition of *The Phoenix*.

26. The English translation is by Charles W. Kennedy, *Early English Christian Poetry* (New York: Oxford University Press, 1963), 231–48. All subsequent English quotations are taken from this text.

27. See chap. 1.

28. Richards, *Chisungu*, 191.

29. C. M. N. White, "Conservatism and Modern Adaptation in Luvale Female Puberty Ritual," *Africa* 23(1953): 17.

30. Cyrus Gordon, *Before Columbus: Links Between the Old World and Ancient America* (London: Turnstone Press, 1971), 20.

31. Franz Boas, *Sixth Report on the Northwest Tribes of Canada*, 60 (London: British Association for the Advancement of Science, 1891), 592.

32. Ibid.

33. Sir James Frazer, "Balder the Beautiful," in *The Golden Bough*, Part 7 (New York: Macmillan & Co., 1919), 1:30.

34. Ronald M. Berndt and Catherine H. Berndt, *The World of the First Australians* (Chicago: University of Chicago Press, 1964), 151.

35. Isidore of Seville, "Phoenix" (Caput VII, *De Avibus*), *Patrologia Latina* 3, col. 462.

36. *Herodotus*, trans. A. D. Godley, II (London: William Heinemann, 1966), 359–60.

37. White, "Female Puberty Ritual," 18–19; Berndt and Berndt, *First Australians*, 152; Frazer, "Balder," 38, 54. A detail from the ritual of fertility cults in Australia helps us to see that the red color of the bird (and the girl) may emblematize blood at the same time that it suggests the sun. Red parakeet feathers attached to fertility emblems used in northeastern Arnheim Land are said by Berndt and Berndt (238) to symbolize "the rays of the sun, the red sky at sunset, or the blood of the Sisters [the Wawalag Sisters who figure in Australian menstrual myth]."

38. Karl P. Wentersdorf "On the Meaning of O. E. *heorodreorig* in *The Phoenix* and Other Poems," *Studia Neophilologica* 45(1973): 33.

39. Ibid., 34.

40. C. T. Carr, *Nominal Compounds in Germanic* (Oxford: Oxford University Press, 1939), 121.

41. Wentersdorf, "On the Meaning of O. E. *heorodreorig*," 35.

42. James E. Cross, "The Conception of the Old English *Phoenix*," in *Old English Poetry: Fifteen Essays*, ed. Robert P. Creed (Providence : Brown University Press, 1967), 136–37.

43. William Shakespeare *The Sonnets*, ed. Hyder E. Rollins, *A New Variorum Edition of Shakespeare* (London: J.P. Lippincott, 1944), 1:52.

44. In an interesting study of menstruation within the context of medieval thought, Charles Wood gives some attention to scientific theory ("The Doctors' Dilemma: Sin, Salvation and the Menstrual Cycle in Medieval Thought," *Speculum* 56 [1981]: 710–27).

45. Each appearance of the word for "blossom" or "fruit" in its nominative plural form, *blēde*, or dative plural form, *blēdum*, occurs in contexts that bring the word into proximity with lines which refer to flowing water. The result is not merely to create an allusion to blood in general but to the catamenia in particular since it is the various forms of *bled-*, which produce the potent image of the blossom or fruit, that recall the verb, *blēdan*. The first suggestion of a pun on *blēd-/ blēdan* occurs in a passage describing the lush abundance of the phoenix's garden. There are two occurrences of forms of *blēd* that appear within three and six lines respectively of a reference to flooding waters (*The Phoenix*, 34–42). The waters alluded to here are the destructive waters of Noah's flood. A second quasi-pun on *blēd* occurs in the key passage about the obviously creative waters, the antithesis of Noah's flood, that flood over the garden once a month (68–72). Here the dative plural of *blēd* appears just one line after a reference to an overflowing stream.

46. Frederick W. Moorman, *The Interpretation of Nature in English Poetry from Beowulf to Shakespeare*, Quellen und Forschungen zur Sprache und Culturgeschichte 95(1905): 41.

47. C. S. Lewis, *That Hideous Strength* (New York: Macmillan, 1946), 62.

48. Ibid.

49. Ibid.

50. C. S. Lewis, "Anthropological Approach," 219–30.

51. The OE lines "ne stanclifu / heah hlifiað ("no lofty cliffs rise") are left untranslated.

52. *Lactanti De Ave Phoenice*, 66.

53. All quotations from the Bible are taken from *The Jerusalem Bible: Reader's Edition* (Garden City, N.Y.: Doubleday & Co., 1971).

54. Blake's introduction to his edition of *The Phoenix*, 16.

55. Arturo Graf, "Il Mito del Paradiso Terrestre," in *Miti, Leggende, e Super-stizioni del Medio Evo* (Turin: E. Loescher, 1892–3), 1:40–41.

56. Blake, introduction, in *Phoenix*, 16; Van den Broek, *Myth of the Phoenix*, 52, 216.

57. Paula Weideger, *Menstruation and Menopause* (New York: Knopf, 1976), 85.

58. Ferdinand von Reitzenstein, *Kröte und Gebarmutter, Geschlecht und Gesellschaft* (Berlin, 1924).

59. Mircea Eliade, *Patterns in Comparative Religion*, trans. Rosemary Sheed (New York: New American Library, 1958), 189.

60. Ibid.

61. Ploss and Bartels, *Woman*, 1:616–17.

62. See Max Bartel's publication of the observations of the missionary C. Beuster in "Zwillingsgeburten bei Basutos," *Zeitschrift für Ethnologie* 18(1886): 36–37.

63. Blake, *Phoenix*, 13ff.; A. S. Cook, ed., introduction, in *The Old English Elene, Phoenix, and Physiologus* (New Haven: Yale University Press, 1919), lii, for example.

64. *Lactanti De Ave Phoenice*, 33, 35; A. Bartlett Giamatti, *The Earthly Paradise and the Renaissance Epic* (Princeton: Princeton University Press, 1966), 70.

65. Howard R. Patch, *The Other World According to Description in Medieval Literature* (1950; reprint New York: Octagon Books, 1970), 3.

66. The OE word "anhaga," meaning "solitary being, recluse," is not in the translation.

67. Berndt and Berndt, *First Australians*, 155.

68. Richards, *Chisungu*, 65.

69. Ibid., 187.

70. Ibid., 188.

71. See note 31 above; and Gilbert M. Sproat, *Scenes and Studies of Savage Life* (London: Smith, Elder and Co., 1868), 93ff.

72. Ploss and Bartels, *Woman*, 1:600.

73. White, "Female Puberty Ritual," 16.

74. Boas, *Sixth Report*, 641.

75. Raum, "Female Initiation," 557.

76. Eliade, *Rites and Symbols*, 42.

77. Berndt and Berndt, *First Australians*, 152.

78. Frazer, "Balder," 22.

79. Ibid.

80. Ibid., 24–25.

81. C. Velten, *Sitten und Gebräuche de Suahili* (Göttingen: Vandenhoeck & Ruprecht, 1903), 100.

82. Sproat, *Savage Life*, 93.

83. Frazer, "Balder," 45.

84. Rev. R. H. Rickard, quoted by Frazer, "Balder," 34.

85. Frazer also cites several examples of suspension above ground from folklore and legend that associate the motif with immortality: the Sibyl was preserved from death by being suspended from the ceiling of the Temple of Apollo; a London girl lived forever hung in a basket from the ceiling of a church and being fed a roll every St. John's Day ("Balder," 99).

86. Eliade, *Myths, Dreams, and Mysteries*, 213.

87. Hutton Webster, *Primitive Secret Societies* (New York: The Macmillan Co., 1908), 46–47.

88. To cite just a few scholars: B. Malinowski, "Magic, Science, and Religion," in *Science, Religion and Reality*, ed. J. Needham (London: Sheldon Press, 1926), 21; Richards, *Chisungu*, 121–23; Arnold von Gennep, *The Rites of Passage*, trans. M. Vizedom and G. Caffee (Chicago: University of Chicago Press, 1960), 81; Eliade, *Myths, Dreams, and Mysteries*, 217.

89. Eliade, *Myths, Dreams, and Mysteries*, 224.

90. Van den Broek, *Myth of the Phoenix*, 52.

91. Margaret Mead, *Male and Female* (New York: William Morrow, 1949), 164.

92. Daniel G. Calder, "The Vision of Paradise: A Symbolic Reading of the Old English *Phoenix*," in *Anglo-Saxon England*, ed. Peter Clemoes (Cambridge: Cambridge University Press, 1972), 1:168.

93. John Bugge, "The Virgin Phoenix," *Medieval Studies* 38(1976): 335.

94. Calder, "Vision of Paradise," 168.

95. Ibid., 167.

96. A. G. O. Hodgson, "Notes on the Achewa and Angoni of Dowa District, Nyasaland," *Journal of the Royal Anthropological Institute* 63(1933): 131–36.

97. Frazer, "Balder," 53.

98. Richards, *Chisungu*, 71.

99. Frazer, "Balder," 97.

100. Mircea Eliade, "The Yearning for Paradise in Primitive Tradition," *Daedalus* 88(1959): 255–67.

101. Ibid., 256.

102. Ibid., 261.

103. This point is, perhaps, best exemplified by a difference in the ritual use of trees among the Shuswap and the Lkungen Indians of British Columbia. Whereas the Shuswap make girls climb trees as part of their menstrual rite, the Lkungen suspend their *babies* in cradles from trees. Boas notes, "When the time of delivery approaches, the parents engage an old man to cut the cedar branch from which the cradle is to be suspended, and five old women to soften the cedar bark to be used for bedding the babe in the cradle" (*Sixth Report*, 572).

104. Eliade, "Yearning for Paradise," 257.

105. Wencelas Sieroszewski, "Du chamanisme d'après les croyances des Yakoutes," *Revue de l'historie des Religions* 46(1902): Part 2, 327.

106. Velten, *Sitten und Gebraüche*, 95.

107. White, "Female Puberty Ritual," 19.

108. Richards, *Chisungu*, 73; Raum, "Female Initiation," 561; White, "Female Puberty Ritual," 16–17; Gennep, *Rites of Passage*, 86.

109. Richards, *Chisungu*, 191, 193.

110. R. Devers, "La rite d'initiation 'Kizungu' dans le Sud de la Lulua," *Bulletin des Juridictions Indigenes et du Droit Coutumier Congolais* 2(1934): 194.

111. Raum, "Female Initiation," 560–61.

112. Ibid., 561.

113. Gennep, *Rites of Passage*, 86.

114. White, "Female Puberty Ritual," 16–17.

115. Frazer, "Balder," 44.

116. Ovid, *Metamorphoses*, trans. Frank J. Miller (London: William Heinemann, 1968), 2:392. ("This bird . . . builds for itself a nest in the topmost branches of a waving palm-tree.")

117. E. J. H. Corner, *The Natural History of Palms* (Berkeley: University of California, 1966), 226.

118. *Encyclopedia Britannica*, 11th ed., s.v. *Phoenix*.

119. Van den Broek, *Myth of the Phoenix*, 183.

120. Ploss and Bartels, *Woman*, 3:20.
121. Harvey Graham, *Eternal Eve: The Mysteries of Birth and the Customs that Surround It* (London: Hutchinson, 1960), 39.
122. Pliny, *Natural History*, 479 (23. 52).
123. Corner, *Natural History of Palms*, 324.
124. Ibid.

Chapter 3. The Conception Sequence

1. Boas, *Sixth Report*, 592.
2. K. Endemann, "Mittheilungen über die Sotho-Neger," *Zeitschrift für Ethnologie* 6(1874): 16–66.
3. Richards, *Chisungu*, 58ff.
4. Eileen J. Krige, *The Social System of the Zulus* (Pietermaritzberg: Shuter & Shooter, 1957), 101–2.
5. Velten, *Sitten und Gebräuche*, pp. 93–101.
6. A. H. J. Prins, *The Swahili-Speaking Peoples of Zanzibar and the East African Coast* (London: International African Institute, 1961), 108.
7. White, "Female Puberty Ritual," 18.
8. Elizabeth Colson, *Marriage and the Family Among the Plateau Tonga of Northern Rhodesia* (Manchester: Manchester University Press, 1958), 288.
9. Ibid., 276.
10. Daryll Forde, *Marriage and the Family Among the Yakö in Southeastern Nigeria*, 2nd ed. (London: Published for the International African Institute by Percy Lund Humphries & Co., Ltd., 1951), 36.
11. R. E. Ellison, "Marriage and Childbirth Among the Kanur," *Africa* 9(1936): 530.
12. Raum, "Female Initiation," 563.
13. Richards, *Chisungu*, 210.
14. Raum, "Female Initiation," 555–56.
15. Oliver F. Emerson, "Originality in Old English Poetry," *Review of English Studies* 2(1926): 20–21.
16. N. F. Blake, "Some Problems of Interpretation and Translation of the OE *Phoenix*," Anglia 80 (1962): 60.
17. Frazer, *"Balder,"* 22ff.
18. Sproat, *Savage Life*, 93–94. Boas's information differs on the precaution. According to his informant, the girl must be shielded not from the sun but from men (593). In either case, impregnation is meant to be avoided.
19. J. H. Breasted, trans., *Development of Religion and Thought in Ancient Egypt* (New York: Charles Scribner's Sons, 1912), 324–28.
20. Sir James Frazer, *The Worship of Nature* (New York: Macmillan Co., 1926), 1:580.
21. Adolf Erman, *Life in Ancient Egypt* (1894; reprint New York: Dover Publications, Inc. 1971), 343. This hymn is said to have been sung by the triumphant soul entering heaven. It is easy to see how a bird, symbolizing the sun as it moves from darkness to light, might have seemed a natural embodiment of the soul to the ancient Egyptians. I raise this idea because in one of its visual representations we see a parallel to a feature of a South African celebrating the triumphant birth of the fertile woman out of the sterile child: the Caffre man who leads the procession while wearing the wings of a bird on his head (see chap. 2). There is in the Ashmolean Museum, Oxford, an Egyptian vase which

represents departed souls as incarnate in dancers, wearing bird head-masks. In a letter to me, Mrs. J. Crowfoot Payne of the Ashmolean dates the vase as pre-dynastic. According to R. J. Rundle-Clark, the dancing figures on the vase suggest "a group of animal spirit dances similar to those carried on by secret societies in modern Africa" ("Origin of the Phoenix," 6). The suggestion is a plausible one, he goes on to explain, because of the "common background of Egyptian and pagan African religion" in, among other things, "fertility and ancestor worship." The phoenix, unifying night and day, death and life, plays a natural role in celebrations of fertility that, after all, connects a dying generation to a new one through the creative powers of women.

22. Richards, *Chisungu*, 194.

23. Forde, *Marriage and the Family*, 22.

24. C. P. Mountford and A. Harvey, "Women of the Adnjamatana Tribe of the Northern Flinders Ranges, South Australia," *Oceania* 12, no. 2 (December 1941): 155–62.

25. Aristotle, *On the Generation of Animals*, trans. A. L. Peck (London: William Heinemann, 1943), 203 (2.5.741ᵃ 10).

26. Ibid. (2.5.741ᵃ 18).

27. Ibid., 171, 173 (2.3.736ᵇ 35, 737ᵃ9).

28. Ibid., 11 (2.2.716ᵃ 14–18).

29. Lucretius, *On Nature*, trans. Russell M. Geer (New York: Bobbs-Merrill Co., 1965), 70 (2. 928–37).

30. Ibid.

31. Lactantius, *The Divine Institutes* 2.10, in *Works*, trans. William Fletcher, vol. 21 of *Ante-Nicene Christian Library: Translations of the Writings of the Fathers Down to* A.D. 325 (Edinburgh: T. & T. Clark, 1871), 1:113.

32. Ibid.

33. St. Thomas Aquinas, *The Summa Theologica*, trans. Fathers of the English Dominican Providence (London: R. & T. Washbourne, Ltd., 1912), Part One, Q 118, A1, Rep. 3.

34. Ibid., Part One, Q 91, A 2, Rep. 2. In a comment on this notion, as applied by C. S. Lewis to the account of the origin of Amoret and Belphoebe (Book Three of the *Faerie Queene*), Alastair Fowler observes, "The tag was still well enough known for Cowley to finesse on it in 'The Parting', *Poems*, ed. A. R. Waller (Cambridge, 1905), 118:

> Thou who in many a Propriety
> So truly art the *Sun* to Me,
> Adde one more *likenesse*, which I'm sure you can,
> And let *Me* and *my Sun* beget a Man."

(C. S. Lewis, *Spenser's Images of Life*, ed. Alastair Fowler [Cambridge: Cambridge University Press, 1967], 48, n. 1.)

35. The Phoenix allusion appears in Job 29:18, and the embryological passage, discussed later in the chapter, appears in Job 10:9–11.

36. Lactantius, *Divine Institutes*, 1:21 (1.7).

37. Lactantius, *On the Workmanship of God*, in Fletcher, *Works*, 2:112–13.

38. Hippocrates, *Regimen*, in *Hippocrates*, trans. W. H. S. Jones (London: William Heinemann, 1931), 1:245.

39. Cf. chap. 2. This point is missed in the notes to those editions I have examined. Hyder E. Rollins notes that "Burned in her blood" may signify burnt alive (*A New Variorum Edition of Shakespeare* [London: J. P. Lippincott, 1944], 1:53).

The same appears in Douglas Bush's note in *The Complete Works,* ed. Alfred Harbage (London: Allen Lane, The Penguin Press, 1969), 1456. G. B. Evans suggests the phrase is a hunting term meaning "in the full vigor of life" (*The Riverside Shakespeare* [Boston: Houghton Mifflin, 1974], 1456).

40. Aristotle, *Generation of Animals,* 109 (1.20.729ª 11).

41. Ibid., 101 (1.19.727ª 21–27).

42. Ibid., 191 (2.4.739ᵇ 21–27).

43. Joseph Needham, *A History of Embryology* (Cambridge: Cambridge University Press, 1959), 64.

44. All quotations from the Bible are taken from *The Jerusalem Bible: Reader's Edition* (Garden City, N.Y. Doubleday & Co., 1971).

45. Pliny, *Natural History,* 2:64.

46. *The Boke of Demaundes . . . between Kynge Boctus & Phylosopher Sydracke.* I read a film copy of the text owned by the Huntington Library.

47. John Lydgate and Benedict Burgh, *Secrees of Old Philisoffres: A Version of the "Secreta Secretorum"* ed. *from Sloane MS. 2464,* EETS, e.s. 66 (London: Kegan, Trench, Trübner & Co., 1894).

48. St. Augustine, *De Genesi ad Litteram, Patrologia Latina* 34, cols. 421–22.

49. "Constantinus Africanus' *De Coitu,*" trans. Paul Delany, *Chaucer Review* 4 (1970): 57.

50. Hildegard von Bingen, *Ursachen und Behandlung der Krantheten (Causae et Curae),* ed. Hugo Schulz (Munchen: Verlag der Uerzlichen Kundschau Otto Emelin, 1933), 102: "Den jetzt gleicht das Weib vom Pfluge durchfurchten Erde, emfängt denn männlichen Samen, umhült ihn mit seinem Blut und erwärmt ihn mit seiner eigenen Wärme. So entwickelt sich der Samen weiter bis der Lebenshauch in ihn gefandet wird und die Keisezeit gekommen ist, wo er hervortreten soll. [As soon as the plough searches the earth of the woman, the seed of the man is fertilized. The woman envelopes it with her blood and warms it. So the seed develops until it comes into its own existence and it goes forth.]"

51. Beryl Rowland, *Medieval Woman's Guide to Health: The First English Gynecological Handbook* (Kent, Ohio: The Kent State University Press, 1981), xvi.

52. Ibid., 58, 60.

Chapter 4. The Birth Sequence

1. Blake, "Interpretation and Translation," 53.

2. Ibid., 53–54.

3. Ibid., 54.

4. Cross, "Conception of the Old English *Phoenix,*" 137.

5. Van den Broek, *Myth of the Phoenix,* 52.

6. James V. Ricci, *The Genealogy of Gynaecology* (Philadelphia: The Blakeston Co., 1943), 20.

7. Ibid., 156.

8. Pliny, *Natural History,* 213 (ch. 8).

9. Ploss and Bartels, *Woman,* 3:112.

10. Blake prefers for *willsele* the translation "pleasant Hall" to "pleasant dwelling" because the latter "disguises that there is a particular reference to human houses and halls here and that the life of the phoenix is being specifically compared to that of man" ("Interpretation and Translation," 54). He, of course, is thinking in terms of allegory, not generation.

11. Ploss and Bartels, *Woman,* 2:736.

12. J. Hooker, "On Child-Bearing in Australia and New Zealand," *Journal of the Ethnological Society of London,* n.s., 1 (1869): 69.

13. Hippocrates, *De Morbis Mulierum,* in *Opera Omnia,* ed. C. G. Kuhn (Lipsae: Prostat in Officina Libraria Car. Cnobbochii, 1825–7), 1:15.

14. Rowland, *Guide to Health,* 23.

15. J. Rueff, *The Expert Midwife* (London: E. Griffin for S. Burton, 1637), 80–81.

16. See chap. 3.

17. Ibid.

18. Adopted by Hubaux and Leroy; S. Brandt and G. Laubmann, eds. in *L. Caeli Firmiani Lactanti. Opera Omnia. Corpus Scriptorum Ecclesiasticorum* 27 (1892); and Marieluise Walla, "Der Vogel Phönix in der antiken Literatur and die Dichtung des Laktanz" (diss., Vienna University, 1965).

19. Appears as an appendix in Blake's edition, 92–93.

20. Hermann Gaebler, "Ueber die Autorschaft des angelsaechsischen Gedichtes von Phoenix," *Anglia* 3 (1880): 516ff.

21. Van den Broek, *Myth of the Phoenix,* 217.

22. Needham, *History of Embryology,* 61.

23. See Ellison, "Marriage and Childbirth," 533 and Isaac Schapera, *Married Life in an African Tribe* (Evanston, Il.: Northwestern University Press, 1966), 233.

24. Gennep, *Rites of Passage,* 44.

25. Joanne S. Kantrowitz, "The Anglo-Saxon 'Phoenix' and Tradition," *Philological Quarterly* 43 (1964): 4.

26. Glimm, *Letter of St. Clement,* 30–31.

27. Blake, introduction, in *Phoenix,* 11; Van den Broek, *Myth of the Phoenix,* 189.

28. St. Thomas Aquinas, *Summa,* Part One, Q 27, Art. 2, Obj. 1.

29. Plutarch of Chaeronea, *Moralia,* trans. Philemon Holland (London: E. P. Dutton, 1936), 297.

30. Needham, *History of Embryology,* 77.

31. From the time of Herodotus, the eagle was used to suggest the size of the phoenix. See Godley, *Herodotus,* 359–60.

32. For example, Kantrowitz, " 'Phoenix' and Tradition," 9; Van den Broek, *Myth of the Phoenix,* 218.

33. Aristotle, *Generation of Animals,* 303.

34. E. S. Hartland, *Primitive Paternity* (London: D. Nutt, 1909–10), 1:309.

35. Robertson Smith, *Lectures on the Relgion of the Semites,* ed. S. A. Cook, 3rd ed. (London: A. & C. Black, 1927), 537.

36. Galen, *On the Natural Faculties,* trans. Arthur J. Black (London: William Heinemann, 1963), 1:vi, 19.

37. Lucretius, *De Rerum Natura,* trans. W. H. D. Rouse (London: William Heinemann, 1975).

38. Sophocles, *Antigone,* in *Three Theban Plays,* trans. Theodore H. Banks (New York: Oxford University Press, 1956), 17.

39. Cited by Eliade, *Comparative Religion,* 256. Eliade has a good discussion of the earth-woman-fertility relationship on 239–62.

40. Shakespeare, *The Complete Works,* ed. G. B. Harrison (New York: Harcourt, Brace & World, 1952).

41. Alexander Krappe, *Études de mythologie et de folklore germanique* (Paris: E. Leroux, 1928), 62. The Old English is not cited by Krappe but may be found in *Bibliothek der angelsächsischen Poesie,* ed. C. W. N. Grein (Kasel: Georg H. Wigand, 1883), 1:316. Above, I have translated Krappe's French rendering into English.

42. Richards, *Chisungu*, 102.

43. See chap. 3.

44. Bruce Lincoln, *Emerging from the Chrysalis: Studies in Rituals of Women's Initiation* (Cambridge: Harvard University Press, 1981), 48.

45. Ibid., 49.

46. Ibid., 45.

47. Raymond Crawfurd, "Of Superstitions Concerning Menstruation," *Proceedings of The Royal Society of Medicine* 9, no. 2 (1915): 52.

48. Two who do are Cross ("Conception of The Old English *Phoenix*," 133) and Thomas Hill, "The 'Swywarena Lond' and the Itinerary of the Phoenix: A Note on Typological Allusion in The Old English *Phoenix*," *Notes and Queries* 23 (1976): 482–84.

49. Cross, "Conception of The Old English *Phoenix*," 137.

50. A. Gavin Hamilton, "Customs of the New Caledonian Women," *Journal of the Anthropological Institute* 7 (1877): 207.

51. Ploss and Bartels, *Woman*, 2:559.

52. Ibid., 577.

53. Sir James G. Frazer, *Pausanias and Other Greek Sketches* (London: Macmillan & Co., 1900), 249.

54. Richards, *Chisungu*, 109.

55. Endemann, "Die Sotho-Neger," 38ff.

56. A. W. Painter, "On the Hill Arrians," *Journal of the Anthropological Society of Bombay* 2(1890):148.

57. For these lines I follow the translation of the Latin poem by Ella Isabel Harris which appears in Cook, *Elene, Phoenix, and Physiologus*, 124–28. Fitzpatrick fails to mention the gifts.

58. Eliade, *Rites and Symbols*, 43.

59. Unpublished communication from Rhodes-Livingston Institute.

60. Blake, introduction, in *Phoenix*, 9.

61. Tacitus, *Annals*, 201 (3. 6. 28).

62. Ronald Syme, *Tacitus* (1958; reprint, Oxford: Clarendon Press, 1979), 2:472.

63. Cross, "Conception of The Old English *Phoenix*," 137.

64. Ibid., 136.

65. Ibid., 133.

Chapter 5. A Reexamination of the Meaning of *The Phoenix*

1. Robert Burlin, *The Old English Advent: A Typological Commentary* (New Haven: Yale University Press, 1968), 32–33.

2. See chap. 1.

3. Ibid.

4. St. Augustine, *Sermones ad Populum*, in *Patrologia Latina* 38, col. 1005, *Sermo* 188 ("Unde *virginem castam* in tot populis utriusque sexus, in tot non solum pueris et virginibus, verum etiam conjugatis patribus, matribusque?"). Translation by Sister Mary Muldowney, *Sermons on the Liturgical Seasons* (New York: Fathers of the Church, Inc., 1959), 19–20.

5. Rufinus Tyrannius, *Commentaries*, in *Patrologia Latina* 21, col. 350 ("Et tamen quid mirum videtur, si virgo conceperit, cum Orientis avem, quam Phœnicem vocant, in tantum sine conjuge nasci . . .?").

6. Rowland, *Birds*, 136. The reference in Albertus Magnus is *De Laudibus Beatae Mariae* 7. 3. 1.

7. "The Canonization," 1. 25, in *John Donne's Poetry*, ed. A. L. Clements (New York: W. W. Norton, 1966), 6.

8. For example, despite their differing approaches to the poem, the man-Christ reference is clear in the conclusions Blake, Calder and Cross reach about the phoenix symbol. In the introduction to his edition of *The Phoenix*, Blake states, "The phoenix represents at first all men who will rise again at Doomsday, then more narrowly all men who will go to heaven, and finally Christ himself" (33). Calder, developing his view of the "kaleidoscopic technique" of the poem's allegory, concludes that the phoenix is the symbol of the "divine" and of the "human" in "one adorned and risen bird" ("Vision of Paradise," 179–80). And Cross's fourfold analysis of the allegorical structure turns up the following results: "The phoenix as the good Christian in his earthly nest is a *moral* or *tropological* interpretation, the bird as Christian in his heavenly dwelling is an *anagogical* interpretation and the bird as Christ is a *typical* or *allegorical* interpretation" ("Conception of the Old English *Phoenix*," 136).

9. Calder, "Vision of Paradise," 168. He quotes Arturo Graf on the patristic tradition of paradise: "Il Paradiso terrestre doveva essere di tale bellezza e magnificenza da vincere ogni piu ardita e fervita fantasia . . . ", ". . . il Paradiso terrestre diventava un prototipo di bellezza" ("Il Mito del Paradiso Terrestre," in *Miti, Leggende, e Superstizioni*, 1 : 40, 42).

10. Calder, "Vision of Paradise," 175.

11. Ibid., 168.

12. There seems to be considerable disagreement about whether Lactantius's poem is Christian or pagan. Among those scholars who consider it an early Christian work are Elizabeth Salter and Derek Pearsall, *Landscapes and Seasons of the Medieval World* (Toronto: University of Toronto Press, 1973), 65–66; Giamatti, *Earthly Paradise and the Renaissance Epic*, 69–70; and Blake, introduction to his edition of *The Phoenix*, 12. Some of those who view the poem as predominantly pagan are Robert Burlin, *Old English Advent*, 29; Emerson, "Originality in Old English Poetry," 18ff.; and H. Leclercq, "Phénix," *Dictionnaire Chrétienne et de Liturgie*, 1939.

13. Jean Daniélou, *The Bible and the Liturgy* (Notre Dame, Ind.: University of Notre Dame Press, 1966), 47.

14. E. O. James, *The Cult of the Mother-Goddess: An Archaeological and Documentary Study* (New York: A. Praeger, 1959), 230.

15. St. Cyprian, *Epistola* 73. 10, in *Corpus Scriptorum Ecclesiasticorum* 3. 2. 785 ("Ecclesia paradisi instar exprimens arbores frugiferas intra muros suos intus inclusit. . . . has arbores rigat quattuor fluminibus id est evangeliis quattuor.").

16. Origen, *Selecta in Genesim* 2.13, *Patrologia Greca* 12, col. 99 ("Qui per divinum baptisma renascuntur, in paradiso ponuntur, hoc est in Ecclesia.").

17. W. P. Friederich, *Die Mariologie des hl. Augustinus* (Koeln, 1907), 255.

18. St. Augustine, *Sermons ad Populum*, in *Patrologia Latina* 38, col. 1005, *Sermo 188* ("Virgo itaque sancta Ecclesia celebrat hodie Virginis partum.") Translation by Muldowney, *Sermons*, 19.

19. Augustine, in *Sermon 186* on the Nativity put Mary's genesis another way: "He created His own Mother when He was with the Father." Translation by Muldowney, *Sermons*, 9. *Patrologia Latina* 38, col. 999, *Sermo 186* ("Fecit sibi matrem, cum esset apud Patrem.").

20. P. Rouillard, "Marian Feasts," in *New Catholic Encyclopedia* (New York: McGraw-Hill, 1967).

21. Thomas Livius, *The Blessed Virgin in the Fathers of the First Six Centuries* (London: Burns and Oates, 1893), 65.

22. Thomas Smith, "The Garden Image in Medieval Literature," (Ph.D. diss., University of Connecticut 1968), 6.

23. In *Liber de Viris Illustribus* 83 (*Patrologia Latina* 23, col. 691), St. Jerome writes: "Methodius, Olympi Lyciae et postea tyri episcopus, nitidi compositique sermones, adversum Porphyrium confecit libros, et Symposium decem virginum, de resurrectione opus egregium contra Origenem." ("Methodius, who was from Olympus in Lycia and was afterwards bishop of Tyre, wrote books of polished and balanced sermons against Porphyrius; he also wrote the Symposium of the Ten Virgins, an outstanding work about the resurrection against Origen").

24. St. Methodius, *Convivium Decem Virginum* 8. 6, *Patrologia Greca* 18, col. 147, ("Ut enim mulier, informi viri suscepto semine, certo mensium orbe integrum hominem concipit partuque effundit, similiter et quis dixerit eos qui ad Verbum confugiant, Ecclesiae utero continue concipiendos et ad Christi similitudinem formam que effingendos certis temporum periodis, beatorum illorum saeculorum cives praestari. Quare astare illam lavacro necesse est, eos generantem qui illo intinguntur. Hoc enim modo et σελήνη (hoc est *luna*) vocatur ea quam circa lavacrum obtinet vis"). Translation by Herbert Musurillo, S. J., *The Symposium: A Treatise on Chastity* (New York: Newman Press, 1958), 111–12.

25. David L. Jeffrey, ed., *By Things Seen: Reference and Recognition in Medieval Thought* (Ottawa: University of Ottawa Press, 1979).

26. Ibid., caption under frontispiece.

27. Hugo Rahner, "Mysterium lunae," *Zeitschrift für Katholische Theologie* 63 (1939): 313–14.

28. Albertus Magnus, *De Laudibus Beatae Mariae Virginis* 4.8.19, in *Opera*, vol. 20 (Lugduni: Caludi Prost., 1651). ("Cant. 4. Fons hortorum, puteus aquarum viuentium. Ipsa enim fons quantum ad communia beneficia quae exhibit omnibus, puteus quantum ad profundas & spirituales devotiones quas suis specialibus subministrat.")

29. Rufinus Tyrannius, *Commentaries*, *Patrologia Latina* 21, col. 349 (". . . per quam scilicet Dominus ingressus est mundum. Dicit ergo hoc modo: *Porta autem quæ respicit ad Orientem clausa erit, et non aperietur, et nemo transibit per eam: quoniam Dominus Deus Israel transibit per eam, et clausa erit* (*Ezech.* 44). Quid tam evidens de conservatione Virginis dici paterat? Clausa fuit ea virginitatis porta: per ipsam intravit Dominus Deus Israel, per ipsam in hunc mundum de utero Virginis processit.").

30. St. Augustine, *Sermones ad Populum*, *Patrologia Latina* 38, col. 1010, *Sermo 191* (". . . ut et corpus majoris ætatis non reserato aditu domus, intus positis præsentaret, et sponsus infans de thalamo suo, hoc est utero virginali, illæsa matris virginitate procederet [Psalm. xviii, 6]"). Translation by Muldowney, *Sermons* 29.

31. St. Ambrose, *Epistolarum Classis* 1. 42, *Patrologia Latina* 16, col. 1126 ("Quae autem est illa porta sanctuarii, porta illa exterior ad Orientem, quae manet clausa; *et nemo, inquit, pertransibit per eam, nisi solus Deus Israel* (*Ezech.* XLIV, 2)? Nonne haec porta Maria est, per quam in hunc mundum redemptor intravit? . . . Haec porta est beata Maria, de qua scriptum est quia *Dominus pertransibit per eam, et erit clausa* (Ezech. XLIV, 2) post partum; quia virgo concipit et genuit.).

32. Albert Magnus, *De Laudibus* 13. 119 ("Bene Maria dicitur porta Orientalis: quia per eam ingressus est in mundum versus Oriens, qui nos visitauit ex alto: & quia per eam oritur in nobis gratia, & patet accessus ad verum Orientem, id est, Christum, qui ortus est ex ea: & ipsa est Principium ortus nostri ad vitam. Porta

autem Occidentalis fuit Eua, quae fuit principium ingressus nostri ad occasum & mortem.").

33. St. Augustine, *De Natura et Gratia* 36, n. 42, *Patrologia Latina* 44 (". . . sancta virgine Maria, de qua propter honorem Domini nullam prorsus cum de peccatis agitur, haberi volo quæstionem: unde enim scimus quid ei plus gratiae collatum fuerit ad cincendum omni ex parte peccatum, quae concipero ac parero meruit, quem constat nullum habuises peccatum?").

34. St. Ambrose, *Expositi evangeli secundum Lucas* 2, n. 9; *Corpus Scriptorum Ecclesiasticorum* 32. 4. 45–46 ("soli Mariae haec salutatio seruabatur; bene enim sola gratia plena dicitur, quae sola gratiam quam nulla alia meruerat consecuta est, ut gratiae repleretur auctore.").

35. St. Zeno of Verona, *Tractatus* 1. 5. 3, 2. 8. 2, *Patrologia Latina* 11, col. 303, 414.

36. J. Romilly Allen, *Early Christian Symbolism in Great Britain and Ireland* (London: Whiting & Co., 1887), 41.

37. Ibid., 45.

38. J. B. Mayor, "Mary (The Virgin)," in *A Dictionary of the Bible*, ed. James Hastings (New York: C. Scribner's Sons, 1898–1904), 3:268–93.

39. Andrea Dal Pino, *I Frati Servi di S. Maria* (Louvain: Bureau du Recueil. Bibliothèque de l'Université, 1972).

40. For this information I am grateful to Daniel A. Brown for letting me read his unpublished paper, "Service to Mary in the Work of St. Odilo, Fifth Abbot of Cluny."

41. Henri Barre, *Prières anciennes de l'Occident à la Mère du Sauveur des origines à saint Anselme* (Paris: P. Lethielleux, 1963), 300–303.

42. St. Augustine, *Sermones ad Populum*, *Patrologia Latina* 38, col. 1011, *Sermo 191* ("Quod miramini in carne Mariae, agite in penetralibus animae. Qui corde credit ad justitiam, concipit Christum"). Translation by Muldowney, *Sermons*, 31.

43. St. Methodius, *Convivium Decem Virginum* 3. 8, *Patrologia Greca* 18, col. 74–75 (Qui autem imperfecti adhuc et tirones disciplinis incipiunt imbui, hi a perfectioribus, ut a matribus, parturiuntur atque formantur, donec et illi maturo partu editi, in virtutis magnitudinem ac decus regenerentur: ac rursus ipsi quoque per idoneum profectum Ecclesia facti, ad aliorum partum educationemque liberorum operam conferanti, uteri, vice, in vase animae, voluntatem Verbi nulla noxa ad maturitatem perducentes."). Translation by Musurillo, *Symposium*, 66–67.

44. Cross, "Conception of the old English *Phoenix*," 133.

45. Ibid.

46. Hill, "The 'Synwarena Lond' and the Itinerary of the Phoenix," 483.

47. Rev. Eric May, "Mary in the Old Testament," in *Mariology*, ed. Juniper B. Carol, O.F.M. (Milwaukee, Wis.: Bruce Publishing Co., 1955), 1:132.

48. J. R. Johnson, "Tree of Jesse," in *New Catholic Encyclopedia* (New York: McGraw-Hill, 1967).

49. Peter Damian, *De Exaltatione Sanctae Crucis*, *Patrologia Latina* 144, col. 761.

50. Mary as *Nidus Dei*: Adamus Persen., *Mariale*, in *Patrologia Latina* 211, col. 523; St. Augustine, *Patrologia Latina* 171, col. 830; St. Bernard, *Patrologia Latina* 185, col. 609 ff.

51. Arthur Watson, *The Early Iconography of the Tree of Jesse* (Oxford: Oxford University Press, 1934), 43–44.

52. E. F. Siegman, "Woman Clothed with the Sun," in *New Catholic Encyclopedia*.

53. Tertulliani, *De Resurrectione Carnis* 13, *Patrologia Latina* 2, col. 811; St.

Zeno, *Tractatus* 16.9, *Patrologia Latina* 11, col. 381; Cyril of Jerusalem, "Catechesis 18," in *Works*, trans. Leo P. McCauley, S. J. and Anthony A. Stephenson (Washington, D. C.: Catholic University of America Press, 1970), 124. St. Ambrose, "On His Brother Satyrus" (2.59), translated by John J. Sullivan and Martin McGuire in *Funeral Orations by Saint Gregory Nazianzen and Saint Ambrose*, trans. Leo McCauley, S. J. et al. (New York: Fathers of the Church, Inc., 1953), 221–22.

54. Calder, "Vision of Paradise," 176.

55. St.Augustine, *Sermones ad Populum*, *Patrologia Latina* 38, col. 1018–19, *Sermo* 195 (". . . manens in sinu Patris, implevit uterum matris. In quo thalamo, id est, Virginis utero, natura divina sibi copulavit humanam"). Translation by Muldowney, *Sermons*, 43.

56. Rufinus Tyrannius, *Commentaries*, *Patrologia Latina* 21, col. 349 ("Huic onim, quem dudum de Patre natum ineffabiliter didicisti, nunc a Spiritu Sancto templum fabricatum intra secreta uteri virginalis intellige").

57. May, "Mary," 106–7.

58. In translating these isolated phrases, I have found it necessary to depart from the Kennedy translation.

59. W. J. Cole, "Mary, Blessed Virgin, II," in *New Catholic Encyclopedia*.

60. Cardinal Newman, *The New Eve* (Oxford: Newman Bookshop, 1952), 19.

61. St. Thomas Aquinas, "In Salutationem Angelicam, scilicet *Ave Maria*, Expositio," in *Opera* (Venetiis: Simon Occhius, 1776), 8:39 ("Non ergo potuit invenire Eva in fructu suo quod nec quilibet peccator in peccatis. Et ideo quæ desideramus, quæ ramus in fructur Virginis. Est autem hic fructus benedictus a Deo, quia sic replevit eam omni gratia.).

62. Noted by Alan W. Watts, *Myth and Ritual in Christianity* (London: Thames and Hudson, 1954), 12. Since this chapter was written, Jane Chance's book, *Woman as Hero in Old English Literature* (Syracuse, N.Y.: Syracuse University Press, 1986) has appeared. On pages 13–34, she focuses on variations in the image of Mary as keys to the unity of the twelve lyrics of *Christ I*.

Chapter 6. Epilogue

1. Victor Turner, *The Forest of Symbols: Aspects of Ndembu Ritual* (Ithaca: Cornell University Press, 1967), 19.

2. Charles Baudelaire, *Oeuvres Complètes*, ed. Y. G. Le Dantec (Paris: Gallimard, 1961), 11.

3. Ernest Cassirer, *The Philosophy of Symbolic Forms*, trans. Ralph Manheim (New Haven: Yale University Press, 1955–57), 2:104–18. Mircea Eliade, *The Myth of the Eternal Return* (New York: Harper Torchbooks, 1959), 34–48.

4. Brown, "Service to Mary."

5. Carol Ochs, *Behind the Sex of God: Toward a New Consciousness-Transcending Matriarchy and Patriarchy* (Boston: Beacon Press, 1977), 68–69.

6. Erich Auerbach, "The Knight Sets Forth," in *Mimesis: The Representation of Reality in Western Literature*, trans. Willard Trask (Garden City, N.Y.: Doubleday, 1957), 114.

7. The French is quoted from Chrétien de Troyes, *Yvain: Le Chevalier au Lion*, ed. J. B. W. Reid (Manchester: Manchester University Press, 1961). The English translation I have used is by W. W. Comfort, *Arthurian Romances* (New York: Dutton, 1967). Lengthy passages will be translated in notes.

8. Maxwell Luria, "The Storm-making Spring and the Meaning of Chrétien's *Yvain*," *Studies in Philology* 64(1967): 576–78 and Tom Artin, *The Allegory of*

Adventure: Reading Chrétien's "Erec and Yvain" (Lewisburg, Pa.: Bucknell University Press, 1974; London: Associated University Presses, 1974), 150, 160.

9. The Jewish Pentecost, at first a feast of harvest, came to signify the giving of the Law to Moses on Mount Sinai. To the church fathers, the feast of the harvest was seen as a figure of the Resurrection of Christ. Fifty days after the Resurrection, the Holy Spirit descended upon the Apostles; this event is celebrated in the Christian Pentecost. The descent in tongues of flame represents the advent of the New Law that embraced but extended the Old Law given Moses. For the Apostles, the descent is a second baptism since only the Resurrection made possible that aspect of Christian baptism which is the grace of salvation. Before the Resurrection only the cleansing of contrition was available in baptism such as St. John could offer: "I indeed baptize you in water unto penance, but he that shall come after me, is mightier than I, whose shoes I am not worthy to wear, he shall baptize you in the Holy Spirit and fire" (Matthew 3:11). St. John was practicing a Jewish rite that was common and well-known, but the effects of the descent of the Holy Ghost did not accompany it. The Christian sacrament had its beginning at Pentecost.

10. E. Tyrrel-Green, *Baptismal Fonts* (London: The MacMillan Co., 1928), 10–11. It is curious that R. S. Loomis, a great scholar of Arthurian legend, should have found the presence of the Chapel so puzzling (Cf. *Arthurian Tradition and Chrétien de Troyes* [New York: Columbia University Press, 1949] 291), for it is quite evident from a detail of the Schmalkalden mural he himself includes in *Arthurian Legend in Medieval Art* (New York: Modern Language Association of America, 1938) that the scene is regarded as baptismal by the fourteenth-century artist who painted it. A glance at figure 162 reveals that the stone upon which Yvain pours water is a font, rectangular in shape and supported by columns. In fact, the unshaded area within the partially shaded border of the rectangular slab suggests that the font is empty and ready to receive water.

11. "I fear I poured too much, for straightway I saw the heavens so break loose that from more than fourteen directions the lightening blinded my eyes, and all at once the clouds let fall snow and rain and hail" (185).

12. Francis Bond, *Fonts and Font Covers* (London: H. Frowde, 1908), 113. Especially noteworthy is the Norman font of St. Mary, Stafford, which not only contains the traditional lion sculpture but also bears the inscription *"Discretus non es si non fugis ecci leones."*

13. Luria, "Storm-making Spring," 581.

14. "Alas! why do I not take my life? How can I stay here and look upon what belongs to my lady? (226).

15. The French is quoted from *Floire et Blanceflor,* ed. E. P. Du Méril (1866; reprint Lichtenstein: Kraus Reprint, 1970), 74–75.

16. *The Romance of Floire and Blanchefleur: A French Idyllic Poem of the Twelfth Century,* trans. Merton J. Hubert (Chapel Hill: University of North Carolina Press, 1966), 76. All quotations in English will be cited from this translation.

17. Possibly related to the turbulence of the spring is a folk belief concerning a certain spring in the province of Damghan, Persia: it was believed that a storm would arise whenever a menstruous rag was cast into the spring. Cf. G. L. Hamilton, "Storm-making Springs: Kings of Invisibility and Protection. Studies on the Sources of the *Yvain* of Chrétien de Troies," *Romanic Review* 2(1911): 359.

18. Line references to the poem refer to *Le Roman de la Rose par Guillaume de Lorris et Jean de Meun,* ed. Ernest Langlois, 5 vols. (Paris: Société des anciens textes français, 1914–24). All quotations from the *Roman* will be cited from this text.

19. Guillaume de Lorris and Jean de Meun, *The Romance of the Rose,* trans. Charles Dahlberg (Princeton: Princeton University Press, 1971), 52. All further references to the *Romance* in English will be to this text.

20. John Fleming, *The Roman de la Rose: A Study in Allegory and Iconography* (Princeton: Princeton University Press, 1969), 96.

21. See H. R. Hays, *The Dangerous Sex: The Myth of Feminine Evil* (New York: G. P. Putnam, 1964), 39ff. and Crawfurd, "Of Superstitions," 49–50.

22. John Gower, *Vox Clamantis,* in *The Major Latin Works of John Gower,* trans. Eric W. Stockton (Seattle: University of Washington, 1962), 198.

23. Ibid., 199.

24. Dorothy Bethurum, "The Center of the *Parliament of Foules,*" in *Essays in Honor of Walter Clyde Curry* (Nashville, Tenn.: Vanderbilt University Press, 1955), 39.

25. Citations from Chaucer are to *The Works of Geoffrey Chaucer,* ed. F. N. Robinson, 2nd ed. (Boston: Houghton Mifflin, 1957).

26. J. A. W. Bennett, *The Parlement of Foules: An Interpretation* (Oxford: Clarendon Press, 1957), 108.

27. Bethurum, "Center of the *Parliament of Foules,*" 39.

28. Donald Baker, *"The Parliament of Foules,"* in *Companion to Chaucer Studies,* ed. Beryl Rowland (Toronto: Oxford University Press, 1968), 360–62.

BIBLIOGRAPHY

Abrams, Meyer H., ed. *Literature and Belief, English Institute Essays (1957).* New York: Columbia University Press, 1958.

Adam abbas de Persenia, *Mariale. Patrologia Latina* 211.

Albertus Magnus. *De Laudibus Beatae Mariae Virginis.* Vol. 20 of *Opera.* Lugduni: Claudi Prost., 1651.

Allen, J. Romilly. *Early Christian Symbolism in Great Britain and Ireland.* London: Whiting & Co., 1887.

Altaner, Berthold. *Patrologie.* Freiburg: Herder & Co., 1950.

Ambrose, Saint. *Epistolarum Classis I. Patrologia Latina* 16.

———. *De excessu Fratris. Patrologia Latina* 15.

———. *Expositi Evangeli Secundum Lucas. Corpus Scriptorum Ecclesiasticorum* 32, pt. 4.

———. *Hexameron. Patrologia Latina* 14.

Aristotle. *On the Generation of Animals.* Translated by A. L. Peck. 2 vols. London: William Heinemann, 1943.

Artin, Tom. *The Allegory of Adventure: Reading Chrétien's "Erec and Yvain."* Lewisburg; Pa.: Bucknell University Press, 1974. London: Associated University Presses, 1974.

Auerbach, Erich. *Mimesis: The Representation of Reality in Western Literature.* Translated by Willard Trask. Garden City, N.Y.: Doubleday, 1957.

Augustine, Saint. *De Genesi ad Litteram. Patrologia Latina* 34.

———. *De Natura et Gratia. Patrologia Latina* 44.

———. *Sermones ad Populum. Patrologia Latina* 38.

———. *Sermons on the Liturgical Seasons.* Translated by Sister Mary Muldowney. New York: Fathers of the Church, Inc., 1959.

Baker, Donald. *"The Parliament of Foules."* In *Companion to Chaucer Studies,* edited by Beryl Rowland. Toronto: Oxford University Press, 1968.

Barre, Henri. *Prières anciennes de l'Occident à la Mère du Sauveur des origines à saint Anselme.* Paris: P. Lethielleux, 1963.

Baudelaire, Charles. *Oeuvres Complètes*. Edited by Y. G. Le Dantec. Paris: Galliard, 1961.

Bennett, J. A. W. *The Parlement of Foules: An Interpretation*. Oxford: Clarendon Press, 1957.

Berndt, Ronald M. and Catherine H. Berndt. *The World of the First Australians*. Chicago: University of Chicago Press, 1964.

Bethurum, Dorothy. "The Center of the *Parliament of Foules*." In *Essays in Honor of Walter Clyde Curry*. Nashville Tenn.: Vanderbilt University Press, 1955.

Bettelheim, Bruno. *Symbolic Wounds*. New York: Collier Books, 1962.

Beuster, C. "Zwillingsge burten bei Basutos." Edited by Max Bartels. *Zeitschrift für Ethnologie*, 18(1886): 36–37.

Bingen, Hildegard von. *Ursachen und Behandlung der Krantheten (Causae et Curae)*. Edited by Hugo Schulz. München: Verlag der Uerzlichen Kundschau Otto Emelin, 1933.

Blake, Norman F., ed. *The Phoenix*. Manchester: Manchester University Press, 1964.

———. "Some Problems of Interpretation and Translation of the OE Phoenix." *Anglia* 80(1962): 50–62.

Boas, Franz. *Sixth Report on the Northwest Tribes of Canada*. British Association for the Advancement of Science, no. 60. London, 1891.

The Boke of Demaundes . . . between Kynge Boctus & Phylosopher Sydracke. London: R. Wyer, 1536. Microfilm.

Bond, Francis. *Fonts and Font Covers*. London: H. Frowde, 1908.

Brandt, S. and G. Laubmann, ed. *L. Caeli Firmiani Lactanti. Opera Omnia*. In *Corpus Scriptorum Ecclesiasticorum*, 27 (1892).

Breasted, J. H. *Ancient Records of Egypt*. 5 vols. Chicago: University of Chicago, 1906.

———. *Development of Religion and Thought in Ancient Egypt*. New York: Charles Scribner's Sons, 1912.

Broek, R. van den. *The Myth of the Phoenix*. Leiden: E. J. Brill, 1972.

Brown, Daniel A. N.d. Service to Mary in the Work of Odilo, Fifth Abbot of Cluny. Unpublished typescript.

Bugge, John. "The Virgin Phoenix." *Medieval Studies* 38 (1976): 332–50.

Burlin, Robert. *The Old English Advent: A Typological Commentary*. New Haven: Yale University Press, 1968.

Calder, Daniel G. "The Vision of Paradise: A Symbolic Reading of the Old English *Phoenix*." In *Anglo-Saxon England*, edited by Peter Clemoes. Cambridge: Cambridge University Press, 1972.

Carr, C. T. *Nominal Compounds in Germanic*. Oxford: Oxford University Press, 1939.

Cassirer, Ernest. *The Philosophy of Symbolic Forms*. Translated by Ralph Manheim. 3 vols. New Haven: Yale University Press, 1955–57.

Charisius, Flavius Sosipater. *Artis Grammaticea*. Edited by Carl Barwick. Leipzig: B. G. Teubner, 1925.

Chance, Jane. *Woman as Hero in Old English Literature*. Syracuse N.Y.: Syracuse University Press, 1986.

Chaucer, Geoffrey. *The Works of Geoffrey Chaucer.* Edited by F. N. Robinson. 2nd ed. Boston: Houghton Mifflin, 1957.

Chittick, H. N. "The Coast of East Africa." In *The African Iron Age*, edited by P. L. Shinnie. Oxford: Oxford University Press, 1971.

Chrétien de Troyes. *Yvain: Le Chevalier au Lion*. Edited by J. B. W. Reid. Manchester: Manchester University Press, 1961.

Claudian. *Phoenix*. In Hubaux and Leroy, xxi–xxvi.

Clement of Alexandria. *The Miscellanies*. Vol. 1 of *Writings*. Translated by William Wilson. Edinburgh: Clark, 1868–69.

Clement of Rome. *The Letter of St. Clement of Rome to the Corinthians*. Translated by Francis X. Glimm, S. T. L. New York: CIMA Publishing, 1947.

Cole, S. M. *The Prehistory of East Africa*. 2nd ed. London: Macmillan, 1963.

Cole, W. J. "Mary, Blessed Virgin, II." In *New Catholic Encyclopedia*, 1967.

Colson, Elizabeth. *Marriage and the Family Among the Plateau Tonga of Northern Rhodesia*. Manchester: Manchester University Press, 1958.

Commodian. *Carmen Apologeticum. Patrologia Latina* 5.

Comfort, W. W., trans. *Arthurian Romances*. New York: Dutton, 1967.

Constantinus Africanus. "Constantinus Africanus' *De Coitu*." Translated by Paul Delany. *Chaucer Review* 4(1970): 55–65.

Cook, A. S., ed. *The Old English Elene, Phoenix, and Physiologus*. New Haven: Yale University Press, 1919.

Corner, E. J. H. *The Natural History of Palms*. Berkeley: University of California, 1966.

Corpus Scriptorum Ecclesiasticorum Latinorum. Vienna: C. Geroldi & Sons, 1866–1913.

Cory, H. *African Figurines: Their Ceremonial Use in Puberty Rites in Tankanyika*. London: Faber and Faber, 1956.

Crawfurd, Raymond. "Of Superstitions Concerning Menstruation." *Proceedings of the Royal Society of Medicine* 9, no. 2 (1915): 49–62.

Cross, James E. "The Conception of the Old English *Phoenix*." In *Old English Poetry: Fifteen Essays*, edited by Robert P. Creed. Providence: Brown University Press, 1967.

Cyprian, Saint. *Epistola 73.10. Corpus Scriptorum Ecclesiasticorum*, 3, pt. 2, 785.

Cyril of Jerusalem. *Works*. Translated by Leo P. McCauley, S. J. and Anthony A. Stephenson. Washington, D. C.: Catholic University of America Press, 1970.

Dal Pino, Andrea. *I Frati Servi di S. Maria*. Louvain: Bureau du Recueil. Bibliothèque de l'Université, 1972.

Daniélou, Jean. *The Bible and the Liturgy*. Notre Dame, Indiana: University of Notre Dame Press, 1966.

Davidson, Basil. *The African Past*. London: Longmans, 1964.

Devers, R. "La rite d'initiation 'Kizungu' dans le Sud de la Lulua." *Bulletin des Jurisdictions Indigenes et du Droit Coutumier Congolais* 2(1934): 193–95.

Donne, John. *John Donne's Poetry*. Edited by A. L. Clements. New York: W. W. Norton, 1966.

Dorson, Richard. *The British Folklorists: A History*. London: Routledge and Kegan Paul, 1968.

Dracontius. "Romulea." In *Fl. Merobaodis Reliqviae Blossii Aemilu Dracontii Carmina Evgenii Toletani Episcopi Carmina Et Epistvlae*, edited by Fridericvs Vollmer. Berolini: Apvd Weidmanos, 1905.

Du Méril, E. P., ed. *Floire et Blancheflor*. 1866. Reprint. Lichtenstein: Kraus, 1970.

Eliade, Mircea. *The Myth of the Eternal Return*. New York: Harper Torchbooks, 1959.

———. *Myths, Dreams, and Mysteries*. Translated by Philip Mairet. New York: Harper Torchbooks, 1960.

———. *Rites and Symbols of Initiation*. Translated by Willard R. Trask. New York: Harper Torchbooks, 1965.

———. *Patterns in Comparative Religion*. Translated by Rosemary Sheed. New York: New American Library, 1958.

———. "The Yearning for Paradise in Primitive Tradition." *Daedalus* 88(1959): 255–67.

Ellison, R. E. "Marriage and Childbirth Among the Kanuri." *Africa* 9(1936): 524–35.

Emerson, Oliver T. "Originality in Old English Poetry." *Review of English Studies* 2(1926): 18–31.

Endemann, K. "Mitteilungen uber die Sotho-Neger." *Zeitschrift für Ethnologie* 6(1874): 16–66.

Epiphanius. *Ancoratus. Patrologia Greca* 43.

Erman, Adolf. *Life in Ancient Egypt.* 1894. Reprint. New York: Dover Publications, Inc., 1971.

Fagan, B. M. *Southern Africa During the Iron Age.* New York: F. A. Praeger, 1965.

Fleming, John. *The Roman de la Rose: A Study in Allegory and Iconography.* Princeton: Princeton University Press, 1969.

Forde, Daryll. *Marriage and the Family Among the Yakö in Southeastern Nigeria.* 2nd ed. London: Published for the International African Institute by Percy Lund Humphries & Co., Ltd., 1951.

Frazer, Sir James. "Balder the Beautiful." In *The Golden Bough,* Part 7. New York: Macmillan & Co., 1919.

———. "The Magic Art and the Evolution of Kings." In *The Golden Bough,* Part 1. New York: Macmillan & Co., 1917.

———. *Pausanias and Other Greek Sketches.* London: Macmillan & Co., 1900.

———. *The Worship of Nature.* New York: Macmillan & Co., 1926.

Friederich, W. P. *Die Mariologie des hl. Augustinus.* Koeln, 1907.

Gaebler, Hermann. "Ueber die Autorschaft des angelsaechsischen Gedichtes von Phoenix." *Anglia* 3(1880): 488–526.

Galen. *On the Natural Faculties.* Translated by Arthur J. Black. London: William Heinemann, 1963.

Gardiner, Sir Alan. *Egyptian Grammar.* 3rd ed. London: Oxford University Press, 1957.

Gennep, Arnold von. *The Rites of Passage.* Translated by M. Vizedom and G. Caffee. Chicago: University of Chicago Press, 1960.

Giamatti, A. Bartlett. *The Earthly Paradise and the Renaissance Epic.* Princeton: Princeton University Press, 1966.

Gimbutas, Marija. *The Gods and Goddesses of Old Europe 7,000 to 3,500 B.C.: Myths, Legends, and Cult Images.* Berkeley: University of California, 1974.

Gordon, Cyrus. *Before Columbus: Links Between the Old World and Ancient America.* London: Turnstone Press, 1971.

Gower, John. *Vox Clamantis.* In *The Major Latin Works of John Gower.* Translated by Eric W. Stockton. Seattle: University of Washington, 1962.

Graf, Arturo. *Miti, Leggende, e Superstizioni del Medio Evo.* 2 vols. Turin: E. Loescher, 1892–93.

Graham, Harvey. *Eternal Eve: The Mysteries of Birth and the Customs that Surround It.* London: Hutchinson, 1960.

Graves, Robert. *The White Goddess.* New York: Creative Age Press, 1948.

Gregory Nazianzen, Saint and Saint Ambrose. *Funeral Orations by Saint Gregory Nazianzen and Saint Ambrose.* Translated by Leo McCauley, S. J. et al. New York: Fathers of the Church, Inc., 1953.

Grein, C. W. M., ed. *Bibliothek der angelsachsischen Poesie.* 3 vols. Kasel: Georg H. Wigard, 1883.

Guillaume de Lorris and Jean de Meun. *The Romance of the Rose.* Translated by Charles Dahlberg. Princeton: Princeton University Press, 1971.

Haddon, A. C. *Decorative Art of British New Guinea.* Dublin: Royal Irish Academy, 1894.

Hamilton, A. Gavin. "Customs of the New Caledonian Women." *Journal of the Anthropological Institute* 7 (1877): 206–8.

Hamilton, G. L. "Storm-making Springs: Rings of Invisibility and Protection, Studies on the Sources of the *Yvain* of Chrétien de Troies." *Romanic Review* 2(1911): 355–75.

Harding, M. Esther. *Woman's Mysteries: Ancient and Modern.* New York: Harper Colophon Books, 1971.

Hartland, E. S. *Primitive Paternity.* 2 vols. London: D. Nutt, 1909–10.

Hays, H. R. *The Dangerous Sex: The Myth of Feminine Evil.* New York: G. P. Putnam, 1964.

Heffernan, Carol F. "The Old English *Phoenix*: A Reconsideration." *Neuphilologische Mitteilungen* 83(1982): 239–54.

———. "A Reconsideration of the Wine Cask Figure in the *Reeve's Prologue.*" *Chaucer Review* 15 (1980): 37–43.

———. "Wells and Streams in Three Chaucerian Gardens." *Papers on Language and Literature* 15(1979): 339–56.

Herodotus. *Herodotus.* Translated by A. D. Godley. 4 vols. London: William Heinemann, 1966.

Hill, Thomas. "The 'Synwerena Lond' and the Itinerary of the Phoenix: A Note on Typological Allusion in the Old English *Phoenix*," *Notes and Queries* 23(1976): 482–84.

Hippocrates. *De Morbis Mulierum.* Vol. 1 of *Opera Omnia.* Edited by E. G. Kuhn. Lipsae: Prostat in Officina Libraria Car. Cnobbochii, 1825–27.

———. *Regimen.* Vol. 1 of *Hippocrates.* Translated by W. H. S. Jones. London: William Heinemann, 1931.

Hodgson, A. G. O. "Notes on the Achewa and Angoni of Dowa District, Nyasaland." *Journal of the Royal Anthropological Institute* 63(1933): 131–36.

Hooker, J. "On Child-Bearing in Australia and New Zealand." *Journal of the Ethnological Society of London,* n.s. 1(1869): 68–75.

Horapollo. *The Hieroglyphus of Horapollo Nilous.* Translated by Alexander J. Cory. London: W. Pickering, 1840.

Hubaux, Jean and Maxime Leroy. *Le Mythe du Phénix dans les Littératures, Grecque et Latine.* Liège: Faculté de philosophie et lettres; Paris: E. Droz, 1939. [Referred to as Hubaux and Leroy in the notes.]

Hubert, Merton J., trans. *The Romance of Floire and Blanchefleur: A French Idyllic Poem of the Twelfth Century.* Chapel Hill: University of North Carolina Press, 1966.

Isidore of Seville. *Etymologiarum. Patrologia Latina* 3.

James, E. O. *The Cult of the Mother-Goddess: An Archaeological and Documentary Study.* New York: A. Praeger, 1959.

Jeffrey, David L., ed. *By Things Seen: Reference and Recognition in Medieval Thought.* Ottawa: University of Ottawa Press, 1979.

Jerome, Saint. *Liber de Viris Illustribus. Patrologia Latina* 23. *The Jerusalem Bible: Reader's Edition.* Garden City, N.Y.: Doubleday & Co., 1971.

Johnson, J. R. "Tree of Jesse." In *New Catholic Encyclopedia,* 1967.

Kaberry, Phyllis M. *Aboriginal Woman, Sacred and Profane.* London: George Routledge & Sons, 1939.

Kantrowitz, Joanne S. "The Anglo-Saxon 'Phoenix' and Tradition." *Philological Quarterly* 43(1964): 1–13.

Kennedy, Charles W. *Early English Christian Poetry.* New York: Oxford University Press, 1963.

Krappe, Alexander. *Études de mythologie et de folklore germanique.* Paris: E. Leroux, 1928.

Krige, Eileen J. *The Social System of the Zulus.* Pretermaritzberg: Shuter & Shooter, 1957.

Lactantius. *Lactanti De Ave Phoenice.* Translated by Mary Cletus Fitzpatrick. Ph.D. diss., University of Pennsylvania, 1933.

———. *The Divine Institutes. Works.* Translated by William Fletcher. Vol. 21 of *Ante-Nicene Christian Library: Translations of the Writings of the Fathers Down to A.D. 325.* Edinburgh: T. & T. Clark, 1871.

————. *Lactantius' Epitome of the Divine Institutes.* Edited and translated by E. H. Blakeney. London: S.P.C.K., 1950.

————. *On the Workmanship of God. Works.* Translated by William Fletcher. Vol. 2 of *Ante-Nicene Christian Library: Translations of the Writings of the Fathers Down to A.D. 325.* Edinburgh: T. & T. Clark, 1871.

Laevius. *Pterygion, Phoenicis.* In *Fragmenta Poetarum Latinorum Epicorum et Lyricorum Praeter Ennium et Lucilium,* edited by Willy Morel. Leipzig: B. G. Teubner, 1927.

Langlois, Ernest, ed. *"Le Roman de la Rose" par Guillaume de Lorris et Jean de Meun.* 5 vols. Paris: Société des anciens *textes français,* 1914–24.

La Ville de Mirmont, H. de. *Études sur l'Ancienne Poesie Latine.* Paris: A. Fontmoing, 1903.

Leclercq, H. "Phénix." *Dictionnaire Chrétienne et de Liturgie,* 1939.

Lewis, C. S. "The Anthropological Approach." In *English and Medieval Studies Presented to J. R. R. Tolkien on the Occasion of his 70th Birthday.* London: G. Allen & Unwin, 1962.

————. *Spenser's Images of Life.* Edited by Alastair Fowler. Cambridge: Cambridge University Press, 1967.

————. *That Hideous Strength.* New York: Macmillan, 1946.

Lincoln, Bruce. *Emerging from the Chrysalis: Studies in Rituals of Women's Initiation.* Cambridge: Harvard University Press, 1981.

Livius, Thomas. *The Blessed Virgin in the Fathers of the First Six Centuries.* London: Burns and Oates, 1893.

Loomis, R. S. *Arthurian Legend in Medieval Art.* New York: Modern Language Association of America, 1938.

————. *Arthurian Tradition and Chrétien de Troyes.* New York: Columbia University Press, 1949.

Lucretius. *De Rerum Natura.* Translated by W. H. D. Rouse. London: William Heinemann, 1975.

————. *On Nature.* Translated by Russell M. Greer. New York: Bobbs-Merrill Co., 1965.

Luria, Maxwell. "The Storm-making Spring and the Meaning of Chrétien's *Yvain." Studies in Philology* 64(1967): 564–84.

Lydgate, John and Benedict Burgh. *Secrees of Old Philisoffres: A Version of the "Secreta Secretorum,"* edited from Sloane MS. 2464, EETS, e.s. 66. London: Kegan, Trench, Trübner & Co., 1894.

Malinowski, B. "Magic, Science, and Religion." In *Science, Religion and Reality,* edited by J. Needham. London: Sheldon Press, 1926.

Marshack, Alexander. *The Roots of Civilization: The Beginnings of Man's First Art, Symbol and Notation.* New York: McGraw-Hill, 1972.

May, Rev. Eric. "Mary in the Old Testament." In *Mariology,* edited by Juniper B. Carol, O.F.M. Milwaukee, Wis.: Bruce Publishing Co., 1955.

Mayor, J. B. "Mary (The Virgin)." In *A Dictionary of the Bible,* edited by James Hastings. New York: C. Scribner's Sons, 1898–1904.

Mead, George R. S. *Thrice-Greatest Hermes.* 3 vols. London: Theosophical Society, 1906.

Mead, Margaret. *Male and Female.* New York: William Morrow, 1949.

Methodius, Saint. *Convivium Decem Virginum. Patrologia Greca* 18.

———. *The Symposium: A Treatise on Chastity.* Translated by Herbert Musurillo, S.J. New York: Newman Press, 1958.

Migne, Jacques Paul. *Patrologiae cursus completus.* Paris: J. P. Migne, 1844 onwards.

Miskimin, Alice. "Britomart's Crocodile and the Legends of Chastity." *Journal of English and Germanic Philology* 77(1978): 17–36.

Moorman, Frederick W. *The Interpretation of Nature in English Poetry from Beowulf to Shakespeare.* Quellen und Forschungen zur Sprache und Culturgeschichte, no. 95 (Strassburg: Karl Trübner, 1905).

Morel, Willy, ed. *Fragmenta Poetarum Latinorum Epicorum et Lyricorum Praeter Ennium et Lucilium.* Leipzig: B. G. Teubner, 1927.

Mountford, C. P. and A. Harvey. "Women of the Adnjamatana Tribe of the Northern Flinders Ranges, South Australia." *Oceania* 12, no. 2(December 1941): 155–62.

Needham, Joseph. *A History of Embryology.* Cambridge: Cambridge University Press, 1959.

Newman, Cardinal. *The New Eve.* Oxford: Newman Bookshop, 1952.

Ochs, Carol. *Behind the Sex of God: Toward a New Consciousness—Transcending Matriarchy and Patriarchy.* Boston: Beacon Press, 1977.

Opland, Jeff. *Anglo-Saxon Oral Poetry: A Study of the Traditions.* New Haven: Yale University Press, 1980.

Origen. *Selecta in Genesim. Patrologia Greca* 12.

Ovid. *Metamorphoses.* Translated by Frank J. Miller. 2 vols. London: William Heinemann, 1968.

Painter, A. W. "On the Hill Arrians." *Journal of the Anthropological Society of Bombay* 2(1890): 146–55.

Patch, Howard R. *The Other World According to Description in Medieval Literature.* 1950. Reprint. New York: Octagon Books, 1970.

Peter Damian, Saint. *De Exaltatione Sanctae Crucis. Patrologia Latina* 144.

—————. *Opuscula Varia. De Bona Religiosi Status. Patrologia Latina* 145.

Physiologus (Greek). *Phoenix.* In Hubaux and Leroy, 2–3.

Physiologus (of Vienna). *Phoenix.* In Hubaux and Leroy, xxxv–xxxvi.

Pliny. *Natural History.* Translated by W. H. S. Jones. London: William Heinemann, 1951.

Ploss, Hermann H. and Max Bartels. *Woman: An Historical, Gynaecological, and Anthropological Compendium.* Edited by Eric Dingwall. 3 vols. London: William Heinemann, 1935.

Plutarch of Chaeronea. *Moralia.* Translated by Philemon Holland. London: E. P. Dutton, 1936.

Posnansky, Merrick. *Prelude to East African History.* London: Oxford University Press, 1966.

Praz, Mario. *The Romantic Agony.* London: Oxford University Press, 1933.

Prins, A. H. J. *The Swahili-Speaking Peoples of Zanzibar and the East African Coast.* London: International African Institute, 1961.

Pseudo-Baruch. *Apocalypse.* In Hubaux and Leroy, xxvii–xxxi.

Rahner, Hugo. "Mysterium lunae." *Zeitschrift für Katholische Theologie* 63(1939): 311–49, 428–42.

Ranger, T. O. and I. N. Kimambo, eds. *The Historical Study of African Religion.* London: Heinemann, 1972.

Raum, O. F. "Female Initiation Among the Chaga." *American Anthropologist,* n.s., 41(1939): 554–65.

Reitzenstein, Ferdinand von. *Kröte und Gebarmutter. Geschlecht und Gesellschaft.* Berlin, 1924.

Ricci, James V. *The Genealogy of Gynaecology.* Philadelphia: The Blakeston Co., 1943.

Richards, Audrey. *Chisungu: A Girl's Initiation Ceremony Among the Bemba of Northern Rhodesia.* London: Faber & Faber, 1956.

Roscher, Wilhelm. *Lexikon.* 6 vols. Leipzig: B. G. Teubner, 1924–37.

Rowland, Beryl. *Birds with Human Souls.* Knoxville: University of Tennessee, 1978.

—————. *Medieval Woman's Guide to Health: The First English Gynecological Handbook.* Kent, Ohio: The Kent State University Press, 1981.

Rueff, J. *The Expert Midwife.* London: E. Griffin for S. Burton, 1637.

Rufinus Tyrannius. *Commentaries in Symbolium Apostolorum. Patrologia Latina* 21.

Rundle-Clark, R. T. "The Origin of the Phoenix." *University of Birmingham Historical Journal* 2(1949–50): 1–29, 105–40.

Salter, Elizabeth and Derek Pearsall. *Landscapes and Seasons of the Medieval World*. Toronto: University of Toronto Press, 1973.

Schapera, Isaac. *Married Life in an African Tribe*. Evanston: Northwestern University Press, 1966.

Schoff, Wilfred H., trans. *The Periplus of the Erythraean Sea*. New York: Longmans, Green, & Co., 1912.

Shakespeare, William. *The Complete Works*. Edited by Alfred Harbage. London: Allen Lane, The Penguin Press, 1969.

———. *The Complete Works*. Edited by G. B. Harrison. New York: Harcourt, Brace & World, 1952.

———. *The Riverside Shakespeare*. Edited by G. B. Evans. Boston: Houghton Mifflin, 1974.

———. *The Sonnets*. Edited by Hyder E. Rollins. Vol. 1. of *A New Variorum Edition of Shakespeare*. London: J. P. Lippincott, 1944.

Sieroszewski, Wencelas. "Du chamanisme d'après les croyances des Yakoutes." *Revue de l'histoire des Religions* 46(1902): Part 2, 299–338.

Smith, Robertson. *Lectures on the Religion of the Semites*. Edited by S. A. Cook. London: A. & C. Black, 1927.

Smith, Thomas. "The Garden Image in Medieval Literature." Ph.D. diss., University of Connecticut, 1968.

Sophocles. *Antigone*. In *Three Theban Plays*, translated by Theodore H. Banks. New York: Oxford University Press, 1956.

Spring, Anita. "Women's Rituals and Natality among the Luvale of Zambia." Ph.D. diss., Cornell University, 1976.

Sproat, Gilbert M. *Scenes and Studies of Savage Life*. London: Smith, Elder and Co., 1868.

Sutton, J. G. G. "The Interior of East Africa." In *The African Iron Age*, edited by P. L. Shinnie. Oxford: Oxford University Press, 1971.

Syme, Ronald. *Tacitus*. 1958. Reprint. Oxford: Clarendon Press, 1979.

Tacitus. *Annals*. Translated by John Jackson. 4 vols. London: William Heinemann, 1931.

Tertulliani. *De Resurrectione Carnis*. *Patrologia Latina* 2.

Thomas Aquinas, Saint. "In Salutationem Angelicam, scilicet *Ave Maria* Expositio." Vol. 8 of *Opera*. Venetiis: Simon Occhius, 1776.

———. *The Summa Theologica*. Translated by the Fathers of the English Domenican Providence. London: R. & T. Washbourne, Ltd., 1912.

Turner, Victor. *The Forest of Symbols: Aspects of Ndembu Ritual.* Ithaca: Cornell University Press, 1967.

Tyrrel-Green, E. *Baptismal Fonts.* London: The Macmillan Co., 1928.

Velten, C. *Sitten und Gebräuche de Suahili.* Göttingen: Vandenhoef & Ruprecht, 1903.

Walla, Marieluise. "Der Vogel Phönix in der antiken Literatur und die Dichtung des Laktanz." Ph.D. diss., Vienna University, 1965.

Watson, Arthur. *The Early Iconography of the Tree of Jesse.* Oxford: Oxford University Press, 1934.

Watts, Alan W. *Myth and Ritual in Christianity.* London: Thames and Hudson, 1954.

Webster, Hutton. *Primitive Secret Societies.* New York: The Macmillan Co., 1908.

Weideger, Paula. *Menstruation and Menopause.* New York: Knopf, 1976.

Wentersdorf, Karl P. "On the Meaning of O. E. *heorodrēorig* in *The Phoenix* and Other Poems." *Studia Neophilogica* 45(1973): 32–46.

White, C. M. N. "Conservatism and Modern Adaptation in Luvale Female Puberty Ritual." *Africa* 23(1943): 15–23.

Wiedemann, Alfred. *Religion of the Ancient Egyptians.* New York: G. P. Putnam, 1897.

Winterbottom, J. M. Unpublished account of Cewa tribe of Zambia. Rhodes-Livingston Institute, Grahamstown, South Africa.

Wood, Charles. "The Doctors' Dilemma: Sin, Salvation and the Menstrual Cycle in Medieval Thought." *Speculum* 56 (1981): 710–27.

Zeno of Verona, Saint. *Tractatus.* In *Patrologia Latina* 11.

INDEX

Page references in boldface type indicate illustrations.